Legal Frameworks for the Protection of Built Heritage in India

Dedicated to

My silent supporter...
My loudest critic...
My friend, my husband,
Prashant
My exploration and research...
Impossible without him

Legal Frameworks for the Protection of Built Heritage in India

Vishakha Kawathekar

COPAL PUBLISHING GROUP
Inspiring for a better future through publishing

Published by
Copal Publishing Group
E-143, Lajpat Nagar, Sahibabad
Distt. Ghaziabad, UP – 201005
India

www.copalpublishing.com

First Published 2020
© Copal Publishing Group, 2019

This book contains information obtained from authentic and highly regarded sources. Reprinted material is quoted with permission. Reasonable efforts have been made to publish reliable data and information, but the authors and the publishers cannot assume responsibility for the validity of all materials. Neither the authors nor the publishers, nor anyone else associated with this publication, shall be liable for any loss, damage or liability directly or indirectly caused or alleged to be caused by this book.

Neither this book nor any part may be reproduced or transmitted in any form or by any means, electronic or mechanical, including photocopying, microfilming and recording, or by any information storage or retrieval system, without permission in writing from Copal Publishing Group. The consent of Copal Publishing Group does not extend to copying for general distribution, for promotion, for creating new works, or for resale. Specific permission must be obtained in writing from Copal Publishing Group for such copying.

The Author hereby warrants that the Work is original work, that it does not infringe any other copyright. The Publisher is not in anyway responsible for any legal proceedings and expense whatsoever in consequence of the publication or alleged publication in the Work of any pirated, libellous, seditious, scandalous, obscene or other unlawful matter.

Trademark notice: Product or corporate names may be trademarks or registered trademarks, and are used only for identification and explanation, without intent to infringe.

ISBN: 978-93-83419-84-5 (Print)
ISBN: 978-93-83419-90-6 (e-book)

Typeset by Bhumi Graphics, New Delhi
Printed and bound by Bhavish Graphics, Chennai

Contents

Preface   *viii*
About the Author   *xi*
Acronyms   *xii*

1. **Heritage: Definition, Quantum and Expanding Definition of Heritage**   **1**
   - 1.1 Introduction   1
   - 1.2 Definitions of Built Heritage   3
   - 1.3 Terms and Definitions Important for Understanding Heritage   5
   - 1.4 Sustainable Use in Context to Heritage   10
   - 1.5 Considerations for Defining Heritage in India   10

2. **Legal Instruments for the Protection of Heritage Across the Globe**   **11**
   - 2.1 Introduction   11
   - 2.2 Heritage Laws Across the Globe   11
   - 2.3 Definition of Protected Cultural Heritage   11
   - 2.4 Grading of Protected Heritage   12
   - 2.5 Administrative Framework for Heritage Management   13
   - 2.6 Powers Acquired Through Heritage Legislation   13
   - 2.7 Power for Compulsory Acquisition and Compensation   14
   - 2.8 Power to Perform Rituals or Continuations of Religious Practices   14
   - 2.9 Power to Control the Use   14
   - 2.10 Power to Intervene   14
   - 2.11 Provisions of Obligations in Heritage Law   14
   - 2.12 Financial Provisions   16

2.13	Provisions for Human Resources	16
2.14	Sanctions for Failure to Conserve the Heritage	16
2.15	Legal Provisions for Effective Protection of Heritage	17
2.16	The Indian Scenario	17

3. The Constitution of India and Provisions for Heritage 19

3.1	Introduction	19
3.2	The Fundamental Rights	19
3.3	Directive Principles of State Policy	20
3.4	The Fundamental Duties	20
3.5	73rd and 74th Amendments to the Constitution	22

4. The Ancient Monuments and Archeological Sites and Remains Act (AMASR) 1958 23

4.1	Definitions of What the Act Protects	23
4.2	Salient Features of the Act	25
4.3	Analysis of the AMASR Act of 1958	26
4.4	Observation and Analysis towards the Provisions of the Act and Its Applicability in Contemporary Times	26
4.5	Ancient Monuments and Archaeological Sites and Remains Rules 1959	33
4.6	Observations and Analysis of the AMASR Rules of 1959	34
4.7	The Amendments	35
4.8	Difference Between the Ancient Monuments and Archaeological Sites and Remains (Amendment and Validation) Act, 2010, and the AMASR Act of 1958	37
4.9	Observations towards the Provision of the Ancient Monuments and Archaeological Sites and Remains (Amendment and Validation) Act, 2010	39
4.10	Heritage, Where Is It?	41

5. The State Acts as per the Corresponding to the Central Act of the AMASR Act 1958 42

5.1	Introduction	42
5.2	Definitions of the State AMASR Acts in Relationship to the AMASR Act of 1958	43

	5.3	Protection of Built Heritage by State Governments in India	59
6.	**Other Acts Aiding to the Protection of Built Heritage in India**		**61**
	6.1	Laws Required Towards Implementation of AMASR Act 1958	61
	6.2	Heritage Protected with Help of Laws Other than Ancient Monuments Act	61
	6.3	Continuum of the Vulnerability of Heritage	70
7.	**The Future Scope**		**61**
	7.1	Changing Perceptions of Protection and Built Heritage in India	72
	7.2	Efforts Towards Protection of Built Heritage in the Contemporary Times	73
	7.3	From Reality to Expectation	75

Annexure 1: Database of the Legal Definition Related to the Built Heritage in Select Countries Across the Globe   **76**

Bibliography   **85**

Index   **91**

Preface

The journey to the book started with Nisar Khan repeatedly telling me that there is hardly any material on the topic. He insisted that the first book on the topic should be simple, communicable and gives an umbrella of reading required to understand legal protection in India.

The book deals with the AMASR Act of 1958 in detail and gives a larger picture about the various legal instruments operational in India.

My interest and quest in the area of "Jurisprudence and Jurisdiction for protection of heritage in India" grew after started working with Prof Nalini Thakur, who very actively was in the subject, experimenting to give holistic and integrated protection to the heritage sites in India. Her engagements with site of Khajuraho World Heritage Site, Kangla Archaeological Park, Mehrauli Archaeological Park, Hampi Cultural Landscapes, Champaner-Pawagadh Archaeological Park and Majuli Cultural Landscape are just few examples which I have studied and researched with her. Her entire effort to look at the sites holistically didn't go well with many authorities as within one site there are so many agencies that operate and bringing them to one platform is indeed a herculean task.

These case studies exposed me to the fact that our understanding of heritage is so fragmented that when she taught us in the Dept. of Architectural Conservation, SPA New Delhi, about redefining heritage; one seldom understood the intensity of the urge, steamed from the fact that our defining heritage through specific windows of understanding needed to be shattered. So every time an attempt to redefine the heritage was made, which went beyond a monument or group of monuments, the existing mechanisms failed. We had to stitch many Acts, agencies, jurisdictions and bring them to a common platform where this effort many a times was seen as activism or unnecessary bothering for implementing agencies. Maximum times the reactions of these agencies would be 'tell us what we need to do and that's it'. The real question then was who will make the effort every time to bridge this gap.

This work also gave me an opportunity to work with a extremely learned lawyer Rajiv Dhawan. Working in his office and PILSAC I realised law is completely a world which I was unaware of. The legislation that is taught in colleges has such definitive meanings and interpretations. Unless somebody understands law how do we achieve protection. This is the place where I understood the meaning of the word 'Jurisdiction'. A word seldomly understood with all its seriousness. My path to bridge the gap between jurisprudence required for the protection of heritage to jurisdiction in which it is provided has been enlightening. Practicalities of understanding a law to implementing it in its spirit is ensured a hard way. Working with him, I did realise that there is a difference between saying 'oh the law does not protect' and evaluating it for its effectiveness. Because every time he argued where has the law failed and I had to run for evidences.

While working in ASI, I started working with Shri A K Sinha. Accompanying him to the site and addressing the challenges of implementation was a daily affair. While smiling, he used to tell "Now take this pen and paper and draw. What you draw we implement, it has to be as per the law and to the taste of a common man". Not all solutions worked, with such heavy military in Red Fort, seldom did my solutions work. Working with his vast experience, the courage to implement, did I understand the meaning of political, administrative and social pressure in which the implementers of the law work.

This resulted in my doctoral research on 'Relevance of Ancient Monuments and Archaeological Sites and Remains Act of 1958 and its applicability in the changed scope and advancements in the field of heritage and its protection". The doctoral research proved that the AMASR Act of 1958 is not a problem as it completely serves the purpose for which it is made. Our expectations from the law has drastically changed and how many amendments are made to the existing law it will have its own limitations. The doctoral research is really an amalgamation of exposures of three stalwarts Prof Nalini Thakur for her strictness to 'Heritage Jurisprudence'. Rajiv Dhawan for his extreme analytical skill towards law and its jurisdiction and Shri Ashok Sinha, also my guide working long in ASI as an implementing officer, who completely understands the strength and weakness of the AMASR Act of 1958.

The book looks at the heritage quantum that is legally protected. It understands how legal protection is provided across the globe. It reviews the AMASR Act of 1958 to what it is articulated to protect. Lists and understands the variations in the corresponding State Acts for protection. It overviews in brief the other Acts through which protection is extended to the heritage of India and concludes giving insights into the reality and expectations from the AMASR Act of 1958.

The book has largely been derived from my education of Architectural Conservation, practicing as a Conservation Architect, working as a Conservation Consultant in Archaeological Survey of India and teaching in various universities on different aspects of conservation. Interactions with varied professionals in the field of heritage on the relevance of the Act are very diverse. There is a divide of views about the effectiveness of the Act. The views expressed by various conservation professionals are largely experiential in a specific context. Hence this query to holistically study the Act and evaluate its effectiveness mainly in reference to the time it is enacted (1958) to the present times of its implementation (2019), a time gap of more than five decades.

Heritage has been perceived as a knowledge realm where all disciplines including politics, administration, archaeology, conservation, architecture, environment, planning, anthropology, ethnography, sociology, economy, law and even a "common man" is an integral part as a stakeholder and has a say.

I wish to acknowledge Rishi Seth for his insistence, patience and persuasion for this book.

I wish to acknowledge the generous support and interactions with experts, teachers, friends and colleagues. I express my gratitude to many institutes where I have worked in different phases of my life. As for my family, they are just a part of me.

Hope this book inspires many to engage into the research in the area of heritage jurisprudence and new thinking required for protection of heritage in India.

About the Author

Dr. Vishakha Kawathekar coordinates the Centre for Cultural Knowledge Systems, and currently teaches the Masters in Architecture (Conservation) programme at School of Planning and Architecture, Bhopal. She has pioneered many researches, and has worked with multidisciplinary teams in the last seventeen years.

Qualified as a conservation architect, she has worked as a conservation consultant with Archeological Survey of India. She has taught in various graduate and postgraduate programmes in the Department of Architectural Conservation, SPA, Delhi; Department of Museology, National Museum Institute, Delhi; and Department of Recreational Architecture & Urban Regeneration at Jamia Millia Islamia, Delhi. She is a key resource person for teachers and professional training programmes related to conservation in India.

Her doctoral research is on "Relevance of the Ancient Monuments and Archaeological Sites and Remains Act 1958 with its amendments and its applicability in the changed scope and advancements in the field of heritage and its protection". Her research now concentrates on Traditional Knowledge Systems and works associated with perception, interpretation and memory. She is a recipient of many scholarships Including ICCROM and V & A fellowships.

She is the principal investigator for many collaborative institutional projects including Heritage Impact Assessment for the Khajuraho World Heritage Site, and Ashapuri Temple Project. She works with many government departments like ASI, tourism, urban development, etc. She has more than fifteen years of experience in collaborative research projects including international projects with Cardiff University, UK; NTNU, Norway; and British Museum, London.

Acronyms

AMASR Act of 1958	The Ancient Monuments and Archaeological Sites and Remains Act of 1958
UNESCO	United Nations Educational, Scientific and Cultural Organization
ASI	Archaeological Survey of India
ICCROM	International Centre for the Study of the Preservation & Restoration of Cultural Property
ICOMOS	International Council on Monuments & Sites
IMP	Integrated Management Plan
INTACH	The Indian National Trust for Art & Cultural Heritage
NCF	National Culture Fund
WHC	World Heritage Centre
WHS	World Heritage Site
NGO	Non-Governmental Organization
PILSAC	Public Interest Legal Support and Research Centre

1
Heritage: Definition, Quantum and Expanding Definition of Heritage

1.1 Introduction

India is a country with a vast treasure of built heritage. Today, there are 3686[1] Centrally Protected Monuments declared as National Monuments under the relevant clauses of the Ancient Monuments and Archaeological Sites and Remains Act 1958. There are around 5000[2] state-protected monuments declared as state monuments under the relevant clauses of their respective state acts. Also there are large numbers of living monuments, which are under the control of Hindu Religious Charitable and Endowment Boards / Waqf Boards, which are regulated by the respective acts. A large number of built heritage is under the ownership of private institutions/individuals. The rest of the built heritage is unprotected.

The built heritage and the continuing traditions are a proof that heritage still has its place in the life and culture of the people. Today built heritage is looked at more as products of culture, where its interpretations have become an integral part to conservation of these structures.

---

[1] The website of Archaeological Survey of India asi.nic.in mentions that at present there are 3650 ancient monuments and archaeological sites and remains of national importance, the website accessed on 18th May 2019. Also the website of pib.nic.in accessed on 18th May 2019 the website of Press Information Bureau mentions the list of 3686 centrally protected monuments/ sites under ASI. This is the information given by Minister of State (IC) for culture Dr. Mahesh Sharma in Lok Sabha on 12th March 2018.

[2] The website of Archaeological Survey of India asi.nic.in mentions that at present there are 3503 ancient monuments and archaeological sites and remains of state importance under the heading of List of State Protected Monuments, the website accessed on 18th May 2019. Not all states are mentioned in the list, hence the general approximation was arrived at.

Hence emphasis is more on values and significance of this heritage and accordingly they become heritage of universal, national, regional, state or local importance.

With technological advancements, the society has also drastically changed. Thus it is more important to understand the meaning heritage has in the present society. They are also subject to potential threats like rapid urban growth, industrial and intensive agricultural activities, growing land prices, encroachments, etc.

The definition of heritage and tools for protection of heritage on an international arena are best understood through the legal instruments towards protection formulated/propagated by the World Heritage Centre of UNESCO. The rise of the World Heritage Organization in recognition of the universal value of the collective heritage is the part of the "Globalization"[3] established on an international basis. The numerous charters produced by UNESCO and ICOMOS refine the conservation philosophy and are expected to reform and update the conservation practice. Charters[4] are formulated to ensure that the World Heritage Sites are maintained on equal standards, and that major monuments and sites may fulfil standard criteria regarding their recognition when entered on the World Heritage list.

---

[3] The term "globalization" is mainly used to describe the process by which business or economic organizations develop international influence or start operating on an international scale. It came to be widely used in the 1980s, to describe the effect achieved by the ability to connect and exchange ideas instantly that would bring to the world. Initially assumed to be about financial processes, studies gradually highlighted its cultural and political dimensions. The cultural dimension of globalization is also termed as 'cultural globalization'. Cultural globalization is about transmission of culture globally, facilitated by the faster communication modes, international travel, leading to increased interactions among people including exchange of books, artifacts and increased tourism. Now cultural values, ideas, attitudes and norms are shared and adopted among people across national borders. This sharing of ideas generally leads to an interconnectedness and interaction between people of diverse cultures and ways of life, which is giving rise to one global culture. It is also argued that this phenomenon is grossly being codified and defined by the global capitalist system.

[4] Throughout the book the general use of the term "charters" is used to denote those documents such as Charters, Recommendations, Guidelines, or Declarations, each drafted to direct consideration to some aspect of conservation and protection of heritage.

Charters provide the insight of the thinking process and the need towards its formulation. After its formulation, the charters are further disseminated to various countries/conservation professionals for its adaptation. Charters become source of information to give proper guidance to the state parties[5] and the conservation professionals to ensure that protected heritage adequately reflect the cultural identity of the place and its inhabitants. They go a long way in establishing the various definitions of heritage as countries ratifying it also have an obligation towards applying it in their national context.

India is the signatory to the World Heritage Convention[6]; hence, the implication and use of various charters, agendas and declarations in Indian context needs to be studied to understand the response of India as a state party to the changed scope and understanding of heritage.

1.2 Definitions of Built Heritage

The biggest challenge for any country is to define heritage. The diversity of heritage that needs protection is enormous and necessary. Every kind of heritage that needs protection may need different mechanism of protection. Hence how to define the heritage is the tricky part. The trends of past years show that the gamut of heritage that needs protection is fast expanding both in type and scale. The progress has been from heritage at building level often recognized as built heritage to large cultural landscape and sites of industrial heritage. Thus the challenge is shall legislation be capable to handle the scale and type of heritage at the same time.

If the definition of heritage is narrow and specific, then aspects like Intangible and contextual heritage are missed. The inclination is to protect the built heritage of the building.

---

[5]States Parties are countries, which have adhered to the World Heritage Convention. They thereby agree to identify and nominate properties on their national territory to be considered for inscription on the World Heritage List. Source: http://whc.unesco.org/en/states parties (accessed 1 December 2011).
[6]UNESCO WHC, 1972, Convention concerning the Protection of the World Cultural and Natural Heritage, Preamble (online). Available at: http://whc.unesco.org/en/conventiontext (Accessed on 30 March 2009)

If the definitions are broad, they are seen to be holistic, but at the same time may lack details about the type of heritage actually protected.

Definition of heritage must reflect the culture and the diversity of its country. As UNESCO states 'that which is inherited; one's inherited lot; anything transmitted from ancestors or past ages'. This goes beyond physical remains from the past to include aspects of culture such as language, spiritual beliefs and intangible heritage. Hence the heritage that is protected should be value based irrespective of the dominant community, favourite political aspiration and monumental scale of the heritage. While defining heritage apart from the professional, academic and legal view perception of the people should be considered.

The definition of heritage dictates the approach to conservation. It decides the course of development in the country, which in turn demands an administrative framework for protection.

Across the globe, the way heritage is defined legally, follows a close relationship to the advancement in expanding the meaning of heritage. A study of how heritage is defined legally by various countries was undertaken. The data from 80 countries was collected in year 2011 (Refer to Annexure 1). The study reflects that there is difference in how the heritage is defined before and after the Convention concerning the Protection of the World Cultural and Natural Heritage, 1972. Heritage laws passed after 1980 follow the definition of heritage as per the convention mentioned above.

The influence of colonization is also seen in the formulation of heritage definitions across the globe. The countries which are colonized more or less follow of predominant nation. After independence many countries including India have not been able to break the path in which heritage is protected. Even when the dominant country has advanced in the way heritage is protected in its own country.

The initial heritage legislation define heritage either as a monument or artefacts and objects of the past. The material aspect of the heritage was of importance. Age of the heritage was critical in evaluating its value and words like relics; antiquities were used to prove its importance.

This era served the definitions of heritage as movable and immovable heritage. This distinction at times has resulted into two separate laws for monuments/archaeological areas and antiquities. Most countries provide a list of monuments that are protected under this act. India follows the same pattern.

Learning may be taken from countries like China and Japan in Asia, South Africa in African continent, United Kingdom and Italy in Europe, Canada in North America, and Australia in Oceanic continent, which have advanced mechanisms to protect heritage in contemporary time.

1.3 Terms and Definitions Important for Understanding Heritage

Below are some of the commonly used terms and definitions used for heritage protection.

(a) Cultural resources

All the tangible and intangible components of heritage

(b) Cultural heritage

In its broadest sense, cultural heritage contains all the signs that document the activities and achievements of human beings over time. This may include historic buildings, structures, sites, city/town/settlement, historic villages, group of buildings, cultural landscapes, historic gardens, historic housing, traditional housing, archaeological parks, vernacular architecture and the intangible aspects like traditions and customs. The concept also includes not only the singular architectural work but also the urban or the rural setting in which is found the evidence of a particular civilization, a significant development or an historic event. It applies not only to the works of great art but also to more modest works of the past, which have acquired cultural significance with the passing time.

(c) Monuments

Architectural works, works of monumental sculpture, painting, elements or structures of an archaeological nature, inscriptions, cave dwellings and combination of features, which are of outstanding value from the point of view of history, art or science. (Article 1 World Heritage Convention)

(d) Groups of buildings

Groups of separate or connected buildings, which because of their architecture, their homogeneity or their place in the landscape, are of outstanding universal value from the point of view of history, art or science. (Article 1 World Heritage Convention)

(e) Sites

Works of man or combined works of nature and man including archaeological sites, which are of outstanding universal value from the historical, aesthetic, ethnological or anthropological point of view. (Article 1 World Heritage Convention)

(f) Historic cities and towns

Historic urban areas, large and small, including cities, towns and historic centres or quarters, together with their natural and man-made environment (Washington Charter 1987). An historic town is a multi-functional organism with residential, social, political and economic activities. Since this is the essence of an urban organism, the historic area should be properly defined, and these aspects adequately considered and administered. Historic towns should compel recognition because of their architectural interest and should not be considered only on the intellectual grounds of the role they may have played in the past or their value as historical symbols. (Management Guidelines for World Cultural Heritage Sites, ICCROM 1998)

(g) Historic garden

Architectural and horticultural composition of interest to the public from the historical or artistic point of view. The term 'historic garden' is equally applicable to small gardens and to large parks, formal or 'landscape'. (Florence Charter)

(h) Archaeological heritage

That part of the material heritage in the aspect of which archaeological methods provide primary information. It comprises all vestiges of human existence and consists of places relating to all manifestations of human activity, abandoned structures and remains of all kinds (including subterranean and underwater sites), together – with all the portable cultural material associated with them. (ICOMOS Charter for Protection and Management of the Archaeological Heritage, 1990)

(i) Antiquity

To include any coin, sculpture, manuscript, epigraph, or other work of art of craftsmanship; any article, object or thing detached from a building or cave; any article, object or thing illustrative of science, art, crafts, literature, religion, customs, morals or politics in bygone ages; fossils and objects of palaeo-anthropological and prehistoric interest; or combination of things, which are of outstanding value from the point of view of history, art or science.

(j) Outstanding value

Outstanding value means cultural and/or natural significance, which is as exceptional as to transcend cultural boundaries and to be of common importance for present and future generations of all humanity. As such, the permanent protection of this heritage is of the highest importance to the nation as a whole. (The World Heritage Operational Guidelines, 2005)

(k) Authenticity

The heritage must meet the conditions of authenticity broadly. The requirements of authenticity are summarized below:

The ability to understand the value attributed to the heritage depends on the degree to which sources of information about It may be taken as credible or truthful. Knowledge and understanding of these sources of information, in relation to original and subsequent characteristics of the cultural heritage, and their meaning, are the requisite bases for assessing all aspects of authenticity.

The judgments about the value attributed to cultural heritage, as well as the credibility of related information sources, may differ. The cultural heritage must be considered and judged primarily within the cultural context to which it belongs.

Depending on the type of the heritage and its context, may be understood to meet the conditions of authenticity if its value, are credibly expressed through a variety of attributes including form and design; materials and substance; use and function; traditions, techniques and management systems, location and setting; and other internal and external factors that shape the heritage. (NARA Document on Authenticity,1994)

The use of all these sources permits elaboration of the specific artistic, historical, social, and scientific dimensions of the monument and/or archaeological site and remains to be examined. Information sources shall be defined as all physical, written, oral, and figurative sources, which make it possible to know the nature, specificities, meaning, and history of the heritage.

In relation to authenticity, the reconstruction of archaeological remains or historic buildings in whole or part is justifiable only in exceptional circumstances. Reconstruction could be acceptable only on the basis of complete and detailed documentation and to no extent on conjecture.

(I) Integrity

The conditions of integrity are as under:

Integrity is a measure of the wholeness and intactness of the ancient monument or archaeological site and remains besides its attributes. The examination of the conditions of the integrity requires assessment of the extent up to which the ancient monument or archaeological site or assemblage of remains is safe enough or is already suffering from adverse effects of development and/or neglect. (The World Heritage Operational Guidelines, 2005)

The heritage should contain the physical fabric and/or its significant features intact. In case the physical features are not intact there should at least be scope for bringing them back to their original condition by way of proper conservation/restoration based upon the authentic sources.

(m) Protection and management

The protection and management of heritage should ensure that its importance from national point of view, authenticity and integrity at the time of protection is at least maintained, if not enhanced, in future.

(n) Boundaries for effective protection

The delineation of boundaries is an essential requirement in the establishment of the protected area and should be identified in a manner that it ensures the full expression of the value and the integrity and authenticity of the monument or archaeological site and remains.

The boundaries to include all those areas and attributes which are necessary for our understanding of its importance as well as those areas which in the light of future research possibilities may be reasonably considered to have the potential to contribute to and enhance such understanding.

There should be sufficient space to accommodate future requirements of the monument or archaeological site and remains, including tourist-related facilities.

(o) Management

The heritage should have an appropriate management plan specifying how best in future the authenticity and integrity shall be maintained.
The purpose of proper management mechanism is essential to ensure effective protection of the heritage for present and future generations. The management mechanism should incorporate traditional technological practices, existing urban or regional planning instruments, and other planning control mechanisms, both formal and informal.

The management mechanism should be so structured as to achieve the following common elements:

1. A thorough-shared understanding of the heritage by all stakeholders;
2. A cycle of planning, implementation, monitoring, evaluation and feedback;

3. The involvement of partners and stakeholders;
4. The allocation of necessary resources;
5. Capacity-building;
6. An accountable, transparent description of how the management mechanism shall function.

Effective management mechanism involves a cycle of long-term and day-to-day actions to protect, conserve and present the ancient monument or archaeological site and remains proposed for protection. Where the intrinsic qualities of an ancient monument or archaeological site and remains proposed for protection is threatened by action of man and yet meets the criteria and the conditions of authenticity or integrity set out above, an action plan outlining the corrective measures required should be prepared and submitted along with the proposal for protection.

1.4 Sustainable Use in Context to Heritage

It is essential to ensure that the sustainable use does not adversely impact the national importance, integrity and authenticity of the heritage. Uses should be ecologically and culturally sustainable. In certain cases human use of the heritage may not be appropriate considering the physical vulnerability of the structure and the building material used.

1.5 Considerations for Defining Heritage in India

Beyond what is already protected through the AMASR Act of 1958, the heritage of India needs defining where all traditions are equally represented and protected ensuring cultural diversity. Many aspects like the size of the monument or the site, its importance, the physical condition of the monument/site, immediate surroundings including if they have any proximity to the other monuments, are there any ancillary structure which are not protected by the list, etc., need to be considered.

The variations occurring due to geographical locations, time period, different builders, architectural styles, size, different typologies including cultural landscapes, intangible heritage, site of underwater archaeology, industrial heritage, etc., shall be equally represented by giving preference to unrepresented cultural resources.

2
Legal Instruments for the Protection of Heritage Across the Globe

2.1   Introduction

UNESCO formulates various conventions from time to time on topics of social relevance. The countries that are signatories to the convention adopt these conventions.

All signatories are expected to adapt to the principle laid in the convention into the law. Every country is expected to adapt into its own legislative and administrative framework. This way harmonization of international and national legal instruments is achieved. It is further disseminated into local level laws. India is a signatory of the Convention "Concerning the Protection of World Cultural and Natural Heritage. The harmonization between the Convention and national law in India is long due. India still follows AMASR Act of 1958. The conservation policies formulated by ASI make some attempts of harmonization.

2.2   Heritage Laws Across the Globe

A study of around eighty countries towards cultural policies and definitions as per their own law is undertaken to drive to the general observations and analysis. The general characterization is achieved many a times deducing the thin odds (refer Annexure 1 for more details). Heritage law states the purpose of the law and gives glossary of definitions of specific terms used. It is within these definitions that the type and category of heritage to be protected is defined.

2.3   Definition of Protected Cultural Heritage

Most countries define their heritage as ancient monuments, archaeological sites, antiquities and relics. Various approaches are there to define cultural heritage. The definition of cultural heritage is achieved either in one way or in combination of any other methods mentioned below:

1. By mentioning the list of monuments of places to be protected
2. By mentioning the values the heritage needs to qualify like archaeological historic, scientific, architectural, etc.
3. By mentioning the demarcation of an area that needs to be protected; it may or may not be protected zone
4. By mention of age of the heritage, for example more than hundred years; this enables extent of heritage by increase in passing years.
5. By mention of termination calendar date. With the termination calendar date with passing years the extent of heritage to be protected does not grow, for example before 15 August 1947.
6. By mention of time scale or chronology, for example Neolithic era

India uses the combination of 1, 2, 3 and 4 for defining its heritage. The international legal instruments vests the responsibility of protection to the government under whose jurisdiction it belongs. Many countries legally acknowledge the sites of universal importance, the world heritage sites as national heritage of their own country.

The national government commits to the legal protection of the site inscribed in the Word Heritage List. If the heritage legislation of the country fails to achieve it, then it may enact a special legislation to do so; for example, the Hampi World Heritage Management Area Authority Act 2002; and Majuli Cultural Landscape Region Act of 2006.

2.4 Grading of Protected Heritage

Most countries do the classification of heritage through grading. The grading of heritage is usually done on basis of the importance or by value assessment. The grading through the importance depends on the legal framework of the country and may differ country to country.

The highest designation in this system is a national monument. In India the designation by importance is at two levels:
- Monuments of national importance
- Monuments of state importance

Recently, India has also seen monuments protected at local levels, i.e. municipal corporations. The system also establishes the priorities of heritage management. System of value assessment stems from the way cultural heritage is defined.

The grading of heritage in many countries affect the property rights, public access, the level of authority, allocation of funds, activities permitted in the site and penalties. This translates the degree of protection accorded to the sites. The issue related to this system is that, many a times, there are monuments of equal importance to the national monuments. But the degree of protection, management and maintenance of sites of equal importance is negligible as compared to the sites of national importance. This issue is prominent in India.

2.5   Administrative Framework for Heritage Management

Ministry of Culture is primarily responsible for the heritage management in many countries. Sometimes, it is also a part of ministry of wildlife and national park.

Ministry of Tourism, Ministry of Youth Affairs and Sports may also share the responsibility of heritage management in few countries.

It is observed that the responsibility of heritage management is transferred from one ministry to other ministry. Yet many countries have a dedicated institutions or an authority to look after day-to-day affairs. Currently, in India heritage management comes under the Ministry of Culture. Archaeological Survey of India is the prime authority for the protection of monuments of national importance.

2.6   Powers Acquired Through Heritage Legislation

Most legislations delegate the power to declare a heritage of national importance. At the same time, many heritage laws also have provisions of removing the heritage from the list of heritage of national importance. This is done through the process of de-gazetting. The decision to protect as well as unprotect the heritage must be made on consultations with the stakeholders and experts possessing specialist knowledge.

2.7 Power for Compulsory Acquisition and Compensation

Most heritage legislations have provisions for compulsory acquisition of heritage properties. The compensations of it is either mutually agreed, or there are legal mechanisms to acquire it.

Within the constitutions of many countries, the protection of heritage is defined as in "public interest". Hence the right of a private owner to use the heritage property may cause harm to public interest. The ownership of the property is thus transferred from private ownership to that of public body.

2.8 Power to Perform Rituals or Continuations of Religious Practices

Most heritage legislations have provisions towards performing rituals or continuation of religion practices in as restrictive ways. The arrangement of building conservation rests with the government, while the practices are performed by the community managed by the trust or organizations.

2.9 Power to Control the Use

Most legislation makes a distinction between the government and the others, for the usages of the heritage properties. The government management authority for heritage has a free hand towards the type of usage and access to the property. Maximum times the control to restrict or provide access to the heritage and its usage for others than the governmental management authority is restricted.

Zones of protection are formulated to protect the heritage in its context often referred to as buffer zones.

2.10 Power to Intervene

Most legislation makes provisions for the heritage management authority the power to intervene. This is done either by totally controlling the property or through shared responsibility where the onus of conservation of the property rests with the government.

2.11 Provisions of Obligations in Heritage Law

Most heritage legislations make provisions of obligation of protecting the heritage. How this is achieved varies from government depending on their legal and administration frameworks?

2.11.1 Obligation to report accidental findings

Most heritage legislations place obligation to report accidental findings on the owner or user of the site.

Generally, all legislations make provisions for requirement of permit to undertake excavations for archaeological or paleontological material and sites.

2.11.2 Obligation to implement and enforcement of heritage law

Most heritage legislations make provisions of obligations towards implementation and enforcement of heritage laws. They are primarily through punishable offences or penalties. The nature of offences varies from country to country. Many countries treat these as criminal offence. The management of heritage property is the sole responsibility of the government. Many countries have a dedicated government body for it like ASI in India.

The heritage law often imposes obligation to the owners for the maintenance of the heritage property. Rules may require an owner to undertake certain works within specified period, or all the heritage management authority to undertake work at owner's expenses.

2.11.3 Obligation for public participation

Very few heritage legislations make provisions for consultation with stakeholders. Few governments do provide for consultations by permitting objections before imposition of regulations of restrictions on heritage property.

2.11.4 Obligation for presentation and information

Most heritage legislations make provisions for presentations of information about heritage property. They are mostly achieved through provision of information boards and brouchers on site.

2.12 Financial Provisions

There is no standard system for provision of finances through heritage legislation. Many heritage legislations provide for funds from the national government. Some heritage laws are also silent about it. The various models of provision of finances are the following:

1. The government allocates the funds annually irrespective of the revenues deposited to the government. The legislation does not allow the heritage management body to keep and put the revenue generated to direct use.

2. Few heritage laws allow the heritage management body to raise money by way of loans. For loans usually a security provided is the heritage property. This acts to risk in case of default in payment.

3. Different forms of tax relief is another method to encourage private sector to contribute to heritage protection. Tax exemptions are usually in form of exemptions in property tax or payment of tax at lower rate.

4. Many a times subsidies are offered towards the cost of maintenance of heritage property.

5. Very few legislations offer tax exemption in subsidies. The provision for finance is dependent on the central government because the legislations were passed in the era where protection of heritage was primarily alone with the central government.

2.13 Provisions for Human Resources

Many heritage legislations have provisions for the employment of staff through civil services; dominantly, archaeologists are the technical experts for the purpose. Other kinds of technical expertise or its services are acquired through contract or through tendering. Common concern expressed across the globe is that decision makers at the topmost higher levels have minimal exposure to heritage issues and knowledge.

2.14 Sanctions for Failure to Conserve the Heritage

Sanctions including fine or term of imprisonment or loss of permit to carry out development works in heritage property are mentioned in the heritage law. The penalties are used to act as a deterrent for unauthorized action. In most jurisdictions the fine and term of imprisonment can only be imposed by the court of law. Imprisonment is reserved for serious violations including deliberate destruction of heritage.

2.15 Legal Provisions for Effective Protection of Heritage

On overview of legal management framework existing across the globe, it is possible to effectively manage and protect the site. For this purpose, it is important to:

1. Identify, categorize and prioritize on the basis of heritage value.
2. Impose restrictions and obligations on the right to use, maintain and conserve the heritage values, the fabric of the property along with its context.
3. Establish the mechanism for planning resources for the management of heritage property for values it needs to be conserved. This includes financial and human resources.
4. Impose sanctions in case of failure to comply with statutory requirements.

2.16 The Indian Scenario

The notion of protection of heritage in India has undergone significant changes.

The process of legal protection was started in India in early 19th century with empowering the government to intervene in case of misuse of public buildings. By third quarter of 19th century, focus has been on combating treasure hunting and regulating the treasures found in accidental digging.

Early 20th century saw the focus on provision for preservation of ancient monuments, to exercise control over the trafficking of antiquities and over excavation; and for protection and acquisition in certain cases of ancient monuments and objects of archaeological, historical and artistic interest. Protection is heavily based on the paradigm of preservation and minimum intervention.

In contemporary times, protection is understood to have two clear aspects: maintenance and management. Management of heritage is inclusive of change and development; the parameter for all decisions based on authenticity and integrity.

Ancient India on the front of 'built heritage' has been far advanced in its approach and thinking. There are architectural treatises, which establish the knowledge systems towards creation of the architecture including the monumental, so are the concepts of '*punahsthapan*' and '*jernodhar*'. '*Punahsthapan*' largely deals with restoration of the built as per the established knowledge systems, dealing with the physical aspects of the monument/structure. '*Jernodhar*' on the other hand deals with physical as well as metaphysical aspects of the heritage. The negative forces leading to the failure of the structures are studied and analysed. Accordingly, the structure was reinstated.

The need of the today is to look back at our ancient knowledge and bring forth the traditional as well as architectural knowledge system to deal with the maintenance and management of built heritage.

3

The Constitution of India and Provisions for Heritage

3.1 Introduction

The Constitution of India governs all citizens of India. The Constitution gives the legal framework for the country. Culture and heritage are an integral part of the Constitution.

The Constitution of India provides every citizen with Fundamental Rights and Fundamental Duties and gives Directive Principles of State Policy. The State includes the central government, the Parliament of India, the government and the legislatures of each of the states and all local or other authorities within the territory of India or under the control of Government of India.

3.2 The Fundamental Rights

In Part IV of the Constitution is laid the 'Fundamental Rights'. The fundamental rights mentioned below have built-in cultural rights:

i. Article 21 gives Indian citizens *"Right towards protection of life and personnel liberty"*.

ii. Article 25 provides *"Freedom of conscience and free profession, practice and propagation of religion"*.

iii. Article 26 gives Indian citizens freedom to manage religious affairs. In Section (c and d) of Article 26 it also provides *"Right to own, acquire and administer movable and immovable property in accordance with the law"*.

iv. Article 29 gives Indian citizens *"Right towards protection of interests of minorities"*. Section 1 of Article 29 states *"Any section of Indian citizen having distinct language, script or culture of its own shall have the right to conserve the same"*.

3.3 Directive Principles of State Policy

In Part IV of the Constitution is laid the 'Directive Principles of State Policy'.

v. Article 49 is for the protection of monuments and places and objects of national importance. Article 49 states that *"It shall be the obligation of the state to protect every monument or place or object of artistic or historic interest, declared by or under the law made by the Parliament to be of national importance, from spoliation, disfigurement, destruction, removal, disposal or export as the case may be".*

Observation: Nowhere the words including heritage, conservation, preservation, etc., are used. The word protection is used in a very restrictive sense of stopping from removal and destruction in turn implies for conservation and preservation. The approach is completely preventive.

vi. Article 51 is for the promotion of international peace and security. In the notes on Article 51, Bakshi (1996) states that *"International treaties do not automatically become a national law. They have to be incorporated in legal system by appropriate law"* [1].

3.4 Fundamental Duties

In Part IV A of the Constitution is given the Fundamental Duties.

vii. According to Article 51 A (f), it is the *"duty of every citizen of India to value and preserve the rich heritage of our composite culture"*. Observation: This acknowledges and preserves the cultural diversity of India, and the word heritage is used in the clause.

viii. Article 246 of the Constitution gives the subject matter of the laws made by the Parliament and the legislatures of the state as per lists in the Seventh Schedule. As per Article 246, the List I – The Union List, the Parliament has the power to make laws; the List III – the Concurrent List, the legislature of the state has the power to make laws;

---

[1] Bakshi P M (1996). The Constitution of India with comments and subject index, New Delhi: Universal Law Publishing Co. Pvt. Ltd., p.74

and the List II – the State List, the legislature of the state has the exclusive power to make laws. The clauses related to the built heritage in the Seventh Schedule are as follows:

List I – The Union List
Clause 67 of the Union List states "Ancient and historical monuments and records and archaeological sites and remains (decided by or under law made by Parliament) to be of National Importance."

List II – The State List
Clause 12 of the State List states "Libraries, museums and other similar institutions controlled or financed by the state; ancient and historical monuments and records other than those (declared by or under law made by Parliament) to be of national importance.

List III – The Concurrent List
Clause 40 of the Concurrent List states "Archaeological sites and remains other than those (declared by or under law made by the Parliament) to be of national importance."

Correspondingly India has a Central Act[2] namely:

The Ancient Monuments and Archaeological Sites and Remains Act, 1958, has been preceded by the Ancient Monuments Preservation Act, 1904, and came into force with effect from 9th August 1958 that purports to be a self-contained law relating to ancient monuments of national importance falling under Entry 67 of List 1 and to archaeological sites and remains falling under Entry 40 in the Concurrent List.

Antiquities and Art Treasures Act, 1972 came into force on 9th September 1972. According to the Act, export trade in antiquities and art treasures are regulated, and smuggling and fraudulent dealings in antiquities and ancient monuments are prevented.

The Public Records Act, 1993 came into force with effect from the 2nd March 1995. According to the Act, the Central Government in the Department of Culture has the power to permanently preserve public records, which are of enduring value.

---

[2]National Law

Of these only the Ancient Monuments and Archaeological Sites and Remains Act 1958 is applicable to the built heritage. Many of the states have their corresponding state acts.

3.5 73rd and 74th Amendments to the Constitution

The 73rd and 74th Amendments to the Indian Constitution brought in a 'local government' system as the third tier of governance with focus on economic development and social justice. The empowerment of the local bodies namely the municipal corporation, councils and *nagar panchayats* through the 74th Amendment in 1992 can have a direct bearing on heritage and urban environment. The Eleventh and Twelfth Schedule of the Constitution list various functions of the local bodies. Among the subjects listed in the Eleventh Schedule are "S. No. 21. Cultural Activities" and "S. No. 29. Maintenance of Community Assets." Most states have either amended their Panchayati Raj Acts, or brought in fresh legislation in accordance with the 73rd Amendment to the Constitution. Similarly, the legislature of a state may, by law, endow the committees with such powers and authority as may be necessary to enable them to carry out the responsibilities conferred upon them, including those in relation to the matters listed in the Twelfth Schedule.

4
The Ancient Monuments and Archeological Sites and Remains Act (AMASR) 1958[1]

In fulfillment of the provisions of the Constitution, the Parliament passed Ancient and Historical Monuments and Archaeological Sites and Remains (Declaration of National Importance) Act 1951 by which all monuments previously protected under the Ancient Monuments Preservation Act, 1904[2], were designated as monuments and sites of national importance. In addition, over 450 monuments and sites located in the former Princely States were included in this list. Subsequently, through Section 126 of the States Reorganization Act 1956, some more monuments and archaeological sites were added to the list of centrally protected monuments. With a view to meeting the changed situation, a comprehensive statute entitled *"the Ancient Monuments and Archaeological Sites and Remains Act, 1958"* was enacted.[3]

4.1 Definitions of What the Act Protects[4]

In this Act, unless the context otherwise requires:

1. "Ancient Monument" means *any structure, erection or monument, or any tumulus or place of interment, or any cave, rock sculpture,*

---

[1]The Ancient Monuments and Archaeological Sites and Remains Act of 1958 (online)
Available at: http://www.asi.nic.in/pdf_data/6.pdf (Accessed on 13 March 2010)
[2]Ancient Monument Preservation Act of 1904 (online)
Available at: http://asi.nic.in/pdf_data/5.pdf (Accessed on 29 March 2009)
[3]Thapar, B.K. (1992). Our Cultural Heritage: A Reappraisal of the existing Legislation and the role of INTACH in its preservation. New Delhi: Raj Press.
[4]Bare Act: The Ancient Monuments and Archaeological Sites and Remains Act, 1958

inscription or monolith which is of historical, archaeological or artistic interest and which has been in existence for not less than 100 years and includes:
(i) remains of an ancient monument,
(ii) site of an ancient monument,
(iii) such portion of land adjoining the site of an ancient monument as may be required for fencing or covering in or otherwise preserving such monument, and
(iv) the means of access to, and convenient inspection of, an ancient monument; in-title of any such owner;

2. "Antiquity" includes –
(i) any coin, sculpture, manuscript, epigraph, or other work of art of craftsmanship
(ii) any article, object or thing detached from a building or cave
(iii) any article, object or thing illustrative of science, art, crafts, literature, religion, customs, morals or politics in bygone ages
(iv) any article, object or thing of historical interest,

3. "Archaeological Site and Remains" means *any area which contains or is reasonably believed to contain ruins or relics of historical or archaeological importance which have been in existence for not less than one hundred years,* and includes:
(i) such portion of land adjoining the area as may be required for fencing or covering in or otherwise preserving it, and
(ii) the means of access to, and convenient inspection of the area;
(iii) any article, object or thing declared by the Central Government, by notification in the Official Gazette to be an antiquity for the purposes of this Act, which has been in existence for not less than one hundred years;

4. "Protected area" means *any archaeological site and remains which is declared to be of national importance by or under this Act;*

5. "Protected monument" means *an ancient monument which is declared to be of national importance by or under this Act.*

Observation: Nowhere the Act uses the term 'heritage'.

4.2 Salient Features of the Act

The Preamble of Act states that the Act is for the *"preservation of ancient and historical monuments and archeological sites and remains of national importance, for the regulation of archeological excavations and for the protection of sculptures, carvings and other like objects."*
The Act has total of 39 sections and the main features of the Act are:

1. *Preamble*: States the reason for the Act and gives important definitions

2. *Ancient Monuments and Archaeological Sites and Remains of National Importance*: Power of central government to declare the monument of national importance and the process associated with it. Criteria for nomination shall be as per the definition. No format, guidelines or parameters associated with identification of monument and site of national importance given

3. *Protected Monuments*: Acquisition rights, rights to enter agreement with owners, purchase rights as per the Land Acquisition Act of 1894, maintenance of monument, protection of place of worship from misuse, pollution or desecration and voluntary contributions towards maintenance of site

4. *Archaeological Excavations*: Excavations in protected areas and other than protected areas, compulsory purchase of antiquities, etc., discovered during excavation operations, and prohibition powers to stop excavation by anyone unless without the previous approval of the central government (ASI)

5. *Protection of Antiquities*: Power to control moving of antiquities and purchase of antiquities as per provisions of the Antiquities and Art Treasures Act (52 of 1972)[5]

6. *Principles of Compensation*: Depends on provisions under the Land Acquisition Act of 1894 and Antiquities and Art Treasures Act (52 of 1972)

---

[5]Antiquities Art Treasure Act 1972 (Online)
Available at: http://asi.nic.in/pdf_data/8.pdf (Accessed on 29 March 2009)

7. *Miscellaneous*: Delegation of powers, punishments, recovery of amounts, power to make corrections, rules to declare ancient monuments, etc., which have ceased to be of national importance

4.3   Analysis of the AMASR Act of 1958

1. Ancient Monuments Act is applicable to ancient monument, antiquity and archaeological sites and remains whose age is above 100 years. It recognizes protected area in a restricted archaeological sense.

2. The AMASR Act of 1958 has declarative and acquisition powers.

3. The AMASR Act 1958 recognizes ownership in three ways: private with regulatory control, government with regulatory control and acquired property under the regime of the Act.

4. The AMASR Act of 1958 has inbuilt provision for the 'list of protected monuments of national importance' protected by the Archaeological Survey of India.

5. The AMASR Act of 1958 delegates the preservation, repairs and maintenance of monuments.

6. The AMASR Act of 1958 acknowledges the living component of the protected monument only in case of religious structures. Protection of place of worship is again restrictive only from misuse, pollution and discretion.

7. Miscellaneous powers including penalties are incorporated in the AMASR Act of 1958.

4.4   Observation and Analysis towards the Provisions of the Act and Its Applicability in Contemporary Times

(1) The Preamble does not state of protecting the monuments in its context, which in turn needs regulating development activity around monuments and sites. It nor acknowledges that the monuments and archaeological sites are constantly exposed to threats like development activities including infrastructural developments, industries, tourism,

etc., and that Act proposes to build-in effective safeguards against threats.

Comprehensive expression need to be updated and used in the preamble as well as in the relevant sections of the Act in line with the various UNESCO Conventions ratified by India.[6]

No guidelines or criteria have been laid either in the Act or in the Rules to qualify the status for a historical monument or site of national monuments objectively. Such a situation has given rise to anomalies. While a procedure has been outlined under the Act (Section 4(1)-(3)) for declaring such monuments and sites under this category, no criterion has been laid down for determining the level of their importance, or the qualifying criteria's to the list of centrally protected national monuments.

The attempt to systematically evaluate its inscription can be seen from the Form B of ASI namely the 'Assessment of monuments and sites suggested for protection', which includes descriptions of the location of the monument including coordinates, topographic features, climatic data and how to reach the site. The form enquires about the name of the monument including alternative names, brief history, importance and outstanding features of the monument/site including reference to sculptures, painting inscriptions, etc. It further asks for published references. It needs elaborate information about the ownership status whether government or private, if private then whether the owner is willing to enter into an agreement and under what conditions. It enquires about its land holdings including area and boundary recommendation for protection. The form also has details to be filled up for utilization of the monument if any, any revenue from endowment, lease, etc. It wishes to ensure liabilities regarding existing staff; minimum staff that may be necessary if the monument is declared protected as well as anticipated expenditure on special and annual repairs. It evaluates if it is recommended for protection as a monument/site of national importance. If so, section under which protection is proposed.

---

[6]UNESCO WHC, 1972, Convention concerning the Protection of the World Cultural and Natural Heritage and UNESCO 2003, Convention for the Safeguarding of the Intangible Cultural Heritage

(2) To avoid any element of subjective discretion, it would be desirable to indicate detailed criteria for protection as a monument/site of national importance in the Act, which constitutes a vital operating part of the Preamble of the Act.

Some examples to illustrate these are the following:

(a) Sites like Red Fort, Humayun's Tomb, Jaisalmer Fort. It is never clear whether the areas enclosed within the site boundary are protected or not, as many individual structures are declared protected and the status of rest is unknown.

(b) The list of centrally protected monuments does not say much. Lack of clear documentation including plans or description leads to subjectivity and confusion.

(c) The list is silent on the usage of the structures unless religious and in use.

(d) Many rituals or functions add value to the site beyond the structure itself over a period of time like Khajuraho Festival, Rath Yatra of Shree Jagannath Puri, etc.; this fact remains inessential or unaddressed.

(3) The definitions of the Act need to be updated as per the UNESCO Convention concerning protection of World Cultural and Natural Heritage of 1972[7] as applicable in Indian context, as we are the signatories of the convention. New areas/fields of research like cultural landscapes[8], under-water archaeology[9], etc., need to be incorporated.

The age-limit factor of hundred years has stayed since 1904 when the Ancient Monuments Preservation Act was first enacted. There are numbers of structures of architectural and aesthetic importance, of less than one hundred years old, which remain unprotected and as such are increasingly exposed to dangers of misuse, damage, or even extinction.

---

[7]UNESCO WHC, 1972, Convention concerning the Protection of the World Cultural and Natural Heritage, (online). Available at: http://whc.unesco.org/en/conventiontext (Accessed on 30 March 2009
[8]The definition was adopted in 1999
[9]The concept shaped around in 2001

Lowering of age limit or the requirement of age limit as a qualifying factor needs to be considered.

The AMASR Act 1958 also defines antiquity (Section 2(b)), which, notwithstanding the hundred year's clause, is fairly exhaustive but excludes fossils and objects of paleoanthropological and prehistoric interest. These have, therefore, to be added under the definition of antiquity.[10]

New categories of heritage like Industrial Heritage, Modern Heritage, Heritage of 19th and 20th Century Architecture, examples of technological marvels, etc., need to be incorporated.

(4) The "List of Protected Monuments/Archaeological Areas of National Importance" needs to be reviewed objectively. The analysis needs to be undertaken as per the geographical locations, historical, social, typological, religious aspects. The architectural values including the scale, construction techniques, styles and knowledge systems should be considered to know qualitatively what is protected and what needs to be protected. The list should also be evaluated for equal representation of heritage, associations, layering and continuity in traditional practices. Now the National Monument Authority did some efforts to categorize the monuments. The broad categories mentioned are:

Category I: Protected monuments/archaeological sites inscribed on the World Heritage Cultural Sites list of UNESCO;

Category II: Protected monuments and archaeological sites included in the Tentative List by the World Heritage Committee;

Category III: Protected monuments and archaeological sites identified for inclusion in the World Heritage Tentative List of UNESCO;

Category IV: Ticketed protected monuments and archaeological sites (other than the World Heritage Sites and sites included in the Tentative List);

---

[10]Thapar, B.K. (1992). Our Cultural Heritage: A Reappraisal of the Existing Legislation and the Role of INTACH in its Preservation. New Delhi: Raj Press.

Category V: Monuments and sites with adequate flow of visitors identified for charging entry fee;

Category VI: Living monuments which receive large number of visitors/pilgrims;

Category VII: Other monuments located in the urban/semi-urban limits and in the remote villages and

Category VIII: Or such other category as the Authority may deem fit.[11]

This categorization seems more towards management decisions and does not address the qualitative definition or equal representation of heritage of India that is much needed.

It is equally important to qualify the "List of Protected Monuments/Archaeological Areas of National Importance" because the range of monuments differs in their importance. The famous Taj Mahal at Agra is one of the Wonders of the World. It is a Protected Monument of National Importance. Similarly, Kos Minar in Punjab is also a Protected Monument of National Importance. Same importance is awarded to both monuments as they enjoy equal status in the list of protected monuments of national importance. A serious thought needs to be given on the categorization of monuments even within the 'List of Protected Monuments/Archaeological Areas of National Importance".

(5) Defining the 'Monument' in its 'Context' is not addressed. The scale ranges from fortified cities like Mandu in Madhya Pradesh, Jaisalmer in Rajasthan to sacred mountains like Sanchi and Caves of Bhimbhetka in Madhya Pradesh. In all cases only few monuments within the entire fortified walls or portions of the sacred mountains get protected, the rest is either protected by corresponding State departments or else rest to the mercy of local governments or left to dilapidate with time. These areas or monuments also form a part of evidence of the heritage protected and are equally a testimony of history.

---

[11] National Monument Authority

This information is vital for the reconstruction of history, archaeology and knowledge systems. These areas have great potential towards archaeological excavations.

The failure to protect the context of the Monument has already resulted in loss of entire layers of history and the vital relationship of the monument to its surround.

Example is the ancient city of Bhubaneshwar. The Lingaraj Temple has many smaller temples in and around the vicinity, and all the temples had a deep relationship to the water tank in middle. Only the Lingaraj Temple and ancillary structures got protected. The prohibited and regulated area was not adequate enough to protect all relationship including that to the tank. Many temples, historic housing and open grounds got lost in encroachment, overcrowding and developments around. The tank deteriorated due to non-maintenance. It becomes a collection point for the surrounding area.

Similarly, loss of vital evidences and relationships can be observed in most cases, few culminating into traffic isles like the Isa Khan Tomb in Nizamuddin, Delhi. Tanks in the vicinity of Khajuraho Temples have also silted and the water collection channels have closed and built upon. The relationship between the intelligent uses of nature to the built is lost. The destiny of Jahanpanah Wall went the same way. In the entire sprawl of constructions and development the wall is lost. Even with various litigations and efforts by the Courts of India, by the state govt. and ASI, only portions of the wall could be recovered. Over the time, the wall lost its very existence[12].

(6) The provision of the Act relating to acquisition of rights in a privately owned protected monument also requires reconsideration. Since no time limit has been indicated in the Act for the owner of a protected monument to enter into an agreement with the central government for the maintenance of the monument (Section 6), repairs are delayed to the detriment of the monument. Also profit gains remain the focus and the sites get transformed drastically where no longer they remain worth the national monument status.

---

[12]Thakur, N. (2000). Heritage of Delhi: The Ground Reality. Delhi: SPA Delhi

Also trend has been seen mainly in state-protected monuments that the protected monuments are first denotified and then put to adaptive reuse. In most cases adaptive reuse means making of a museum, exhibition hall, a haat or heritage hotels. Experimentation to giving back these structures to the town with uses of public interest is missing.

There are past instances where the handing over of a particular monument to the Centre depended upon the interest and will of the owner of the property. Many a times only a portion of the property is shared, again reiterating the issue of protection without the context, compromising one of the layers of history and knowledge system. Alternative mechanism like special designation allotted to such monuments will ensure safety; conservation could be regulated and forced upon; for example, Jama Masjid, Delhi; Amber Fort, Rajasthan.

(7) Past experience has shown that agreements are very often violated as the monuments involved are in religious use. Permissible customary religious observances are extended beyond limits leading to unauthorized constructions. The conditions of agreement have to be re-examined with a realistic approach within the framework of principles of conservation. Informed community participation is necessary to curb efforts. The conditions of agreement have to be re-examined with a realistic approach within the framework of principles of conservation.

(8) Under the provisions of the Act, agricultural practices to the depth of one meter are permitted. With modernization of agricultural practices, came in use of machines, fertilizers and seepage of water. These prove detrimental to the archaeological remains underground which are at stake. Also transformation of traditional agricultural practice stakes the value of the site for losing its importance. Vandalism is another threat for illicit trafficking or for building materials, for example Hampi cultural landscape area[13].

(9) Heritage impact assessments and no objection certificate should be obtained for large infrastructural and development projects. Any adaptive reuse or provision of tourist infrastructure facilities should also

---

[13]Thakur N. (2006), Integrated Management Plan for Hampi, New Delhi: Archaeological Survey of India

be evaluated on Heritage Impact Assessment where the importance of the site is compromised on. Studies across the world have proved the danger of unnecessary infused development that eradicates the culture of the place totally.

(10) Protection of monuments and archaeological sites needs to be strengthened. Multiplicity of responsible agencies and overlapping decision by various agencies without information or consent of ASI officials needs to be resolved.

4.5 Ancient Monuments and Archaeological Sites and Remains Rules 1959

In exercise of the powers conferred by Section 38 of the Ancient Monuments and Archaeological Sites and Remains Act, 1958 (24 of 1958), the central government hereby makes the following rules, the same having been previously published in the Gazette of India, Part II-Section 3-Sub-Section (ii), dated the 8th August, 1959, as required by sub-section (1) of the said section. The rules deal with construction, copying, filming, mining operation, prohibited and regulated areas for the purpose of mining and construction, licenses, rules towards keeping the monuments open, fees, transfer of ownership, antiquities and movement of antiquities, etc.[14]

The Rules consists of nine chapters concerned with:

(a) *Access to protected monuments* including timings of monuments to be opened and closed, entrance fee, holding of meetings in monument, etc.

(b) *Construction and other operations* including excavation in protected area include procedures to acquire permissions and terms and conditions to be followed.

(c) *Excavation in unprotected areas* includes procedures for intimation and approval from the central government.

---

[14]Dr Alok Tripathi, The Ancient Monuments and Archaeological Sites and Remains Act, 1958 (with rules, amendments, notification and orders), Sundeep Prakashan, Delhi, 2007, pp. 193, 194

(d) *Report on excavated antiquities of an archaeological officer* includes a form of report, etc.

(e) *Moving of antiquities from certain areas* includes procedures for application, grant or refusal of permission

(f) *Mining operations and construction near protected monuments* includes procedures for notice of intentions, declaration of prohibited and regulated areas, application for license, grant or refusal, cancellation of license and removal of unauthorized buildings

(g) *Copying and filming of protected monuments* including procedures to acquire permissions and terms and conditions to be followed

(h) Miscellaneous

4.6 Observations and Analysis of the AMASR Rules of 1959

The AMASR Rules of 1959 are for the administrative and the functional requirements of the law.

1. In many clauses, changing technology and monetary capabilities/expenses need to be considered.

2. Rule 7 states that no protected monument shall be used for the purpose of holding any meeting, reception, party, conference or entertainment except under and in accordance with the permission in writing granted by the central government.

3. Recognized religious usage or custom is, however, permissible. The discretion, therefore, lies with government to permit any kind of usage. Experience has shown that often requests are made for holding cultural festivals or such activities, which are not in consonance with its original use. The publicity and filming media poses a similar threat.

4. Rules 31, 33 are for declaring certain areas near or adjoining a protected monument to be 'a prohibited or a regulated area' mainly for mining and construction. There is no mention or safeguard against any

industrial or other development activity, which may adversely affect the monument. These are for regulating new constructions in the close vicinity of monuments to establish compatibility and visual linkages with the site.

The rules are in process of substantial modification for the contemporary operation of the Act. The Archaeological Survey of India has prepared draft guidelines on the Protection of Ancient Monuments Archaeological Sites and Remains: for grant of permission for illumination of centrally protected ancient monuments, archaeological sites and remains; for sound and light show at the centrally protected monuments, archaeological sites and remains; for photographers to operate within the precincts of centrally protected monuments; for issue of license for videography and filming at the protected monuments; for grant of permission for organizing cultural programs at the centrally protected monuments and for removal of encroachments from the centrally protected monuments.

4.7 The Amendments

4.7.1 The Amendment of 1992

The prohibited area and regulated area of 100 m and 200 m were declared for few monuments including Fatehpur Sikri, Agra; Mahabalipuram; Golkonda Fort, Hyderabad; Thousand Pillar Temple, Hanamkonda, Dist. Warangal; Sher Shah Tomb, Sasaram; Rock Edict of Asoka, Kopbal, Dist. Raichur; Fort Wall, Bijapur; Gomateshwar Statue, Shravanabelagola; Elephanta Caves, Gharapuri, Dist. Kolaba. But via Gazette notification Part II – Section 3 – sub-section (ii) July 4, 1992, the area up to 100 m from the protected limit and further beyond it up to 200 m near or adjoining protected monuments was declared as prohibited and regulated area for purposes of both mining operation and construction as per the Rule 32 of the Ancient Monuments and Archaeological Sites and Remains Rule of 1959.

This is a thumb rule applicable for all sites, in continuation of policy for fencing of monuments and ignores the context completely. It does not consider the scale and size of the monuments. With no proper documentation notified leads to subjectivity giving rise to more disputes than solutions. With monuments in close proximity, overlapping areas lead to no space even for infrastructural developments, e.g. Ahmedabad Fort, city of Orchha. This amendment though with all its shortcomings still acted as a boon for many sites from being encroached.

The amendment is necessary to protect the immediate surrounds which has the maximum impact on the life of the people residing around it. Change and development is inevitable for any living culture and well-being of the society. The amendments impact the basic need of the people residing around it. The AMASR (Amendment and Validation) Act 2010 has tried to address these issues. The new Amendments and Validation need to be closely monitored and reviewed for its impact and successful implementation.

4.7.2 Other Amendments

Amendments towards keeping the monuments open, fees, etc., are made from time to time. For the purpose of fee structure, there are two categories of monuments:

Category A: World Heritage Sites
Category B: Protected monuments apart from WHS

For the categorization of monuments into World Heritage sites and other national monuments, application needs to be studied in other spheres of protection and conservation also.

The notification dated 31st July 2015 grants licenses to filming on payment. This fee also differs depending on whether the filming is to be done on category A or B monument.

4.7.3 The Ancient Monuments and Archaeological Sites and Remains (Amendment and Validation) Act, 2010[15]

The central government has enacted the Ancient Monuments and Archaeological Sites and Remains (Amendment and Validation) Act, 2010, to make the Ancient Monuments and Archaeological

---

[15]The Ancient Monuments and Archaeological Sites and Remains (Amendment and Validation) Act, 2010 (online). Available at: http://www.asi.nic.in/minutes/AMASR_Act2010_Gazette_Notification. PDF (Accessed on 24 Dec 2011)

Sites and Remains Act, 1958, more effective to safeguard the interest of the ancient monuments and archaeological sites and remains, declared as of national importance. The Act has come into force with immediate effect. The basic definitions remain the same as per the Ancient Monuments and Archaeological Sites and Remains Act 1958 updated to the Ancient Monuments and Archaeological Sites and Remains (Amendment and Validation) Act, 2010.

4.8 Difference Between the Ancient Monuments and Archaeological Sites and Remains (Amendment and Validation) Act, 2010, from the AMASR Act of 1958

The primary differences from the parent Act are:

1. Minimum *'prohibited area'* and *'regulated area'* limits of the protected monuments and protected areas fixed as 100 m and 200 m, respectively, which could be further extended on the basis of gradation and classification.

2. No *'construction'* of any public project or of any other nature is permitted in the *'prohibited area'*.

3. *'National Monument Authority'* is to be constituted, headed by whole-time chairperson and ten members (five whole-time and five part-time), from fields of archaeology, country and town planning, architecture, heritage, conservation architecture or law.

4. *'Competent Authority'* to be specified by the central government for receiving and granting permissions for construction-related activities in the *'prohibited areas'* and *'regulated areas'* of the protected monuments and protected areas.

5. *'Construction'*, *'Reconstruction'*, *'Repair'* and *'Renovation'* defined.

6. Grading and classification of protected monuments and areas to be carried out by the *'National Monument Authority'*.

7. Permission for *'repair'* and *'renovation'* in the *'prohibited areas'* of the protected monuments and protected areas may be granted

by the *'Competent Authority'* on recommendations of the *'National Monument Authority'*, provided the structure is pre-1992 or permission for its construction had been granted by the ASI. No permission for *'construction'* or *'reconstruction'* in *'prohibited areas'* of protected monuments and protected areas may be granted.

8. Permission for *'construction'*, *'reconstruction'*, *'renovation'* and *'repair'* may be granted in the *'regulated area'* by the 'competent authority' on the basis of *'heritage byelaws'* to be prepared for each protected monument and protected area and on the recommendation of the *'National Monument Authority'*.

9. Till such time the *'National Monument Authority'* is constituted, *'competent authority'* specified and *'heritage byelaws'* framed, all construction-related activities in the 300 m area (*'prohibited'* and *'regulated'* areas) of protected monuments and protected areas, shall remain frozen.

10. Heritage controls such as elevation, façade, drainage system, road and service infrastructure (including portable toilets, school building, hospitals, electric polls, water and sewer pipe-line) to be specified in the *'heritage byelaws'* in consultation with INTACH or other such expert heritage bodies.

11. *'Heritage byelaws'* in respect of each protected monument and protected area to be kept in public domain.

12. Penalty for causing damage, alteration, misuse and other acts of similar nature at protected monument and protected areas enhanced from three months to two years and fine of rupees five thousand to one lakh or both.

13. Penalty for undertaking *'construction'*-related activities unauthorized in the *'prohibited areas'* and *'regulated areas'* of protected monuments and protected areas provides with imprisonment extendable to two years or with fine, which may extend to one lakh rupees or both.

14. Surveys of *'prohibited areas'* and *'regulated areas'* of protected monuments and protected areas to be carried out for the purpose of detailed site plans.

15. Provision has been made to identify unauthorized constructions in the '*prohibited area*' and '*regulated area*' after the 16th day of June, 1992.

16. Ex-post-facto permissions granted for '*construction*' in the '*prohibited area*' of the protected monuments and protected areas on the recommendation of the '*Expert Advisory Committee*' or '*Advisory Committee*', held as invalid.

4.9 Observations towards the Provision of the Ancient Monuments and Archaeological Sites and Remains (Amendment and Validation) Act, 2010

(1) The basic definitions of what is protected under the Act remain the same. To the same the protection above ground and below ground for the same monument is extended.

(2) '*Construction*' has a restrictive meaning as a new construction or maintenance of public amenities and promotional structures. No guidelines are prescribed for undertaking such facilities, or establishing its necessity as public amenity. Many a times they are large projects like highways, metro, etc. These are bound to impact the monuments.

(3) Initially no '*construction*' of any public project or of any other nature is permitted in the '*prohibited area*'. The amendment to the Act further dilutes the restriction of prohibited area to allow public works or constructions under the central government. This should be a cause of worry because the cap of prohibited area is important to protect the foundations of the monuments or potential archaeological sites.

(4) National Monuments Authority (NMA) has so far not noticed very few byelaws for any protected monuments and protected area declared as of national importance. Preparation of heritage byelaws for all centrally protected monuments is under process. On web search only the following byelaws are seen mainly for Delhi and Lucknow:

1. Heritage byelaws for Khair-ul-Manazil and Sher Shah Gate, Delhi
2. Heritage byelaws for Nizamuddin Basti Group of Monuments, Delhi
3. Heritage byelaws for Humayun's Tomb – Sunder Nursery – Batashewala Group of Monuments, Delhi

4. Heritage byelaws for Purana Qila, Delhi
5. Heritage byelaws for Amjad Ali Shah's Mausoleum at Hazratganj, Lucknow
6. Amzad Ali Shah ka Maqbara, Lucknow

(5) Number of government agencies are involved in the process of preparing the byelaws till their notification, and the volume of work is very large, time limit is neither fixed nor for notifying the heritage byelaws.

(6) Agencies trusted to work on ground also have a voluminous work. No priorities have been designated. No information is available on public domain; hence, capacity to handle all work at a go and the time factor are primary reasons for the delay.

(7) Heritage byelaws are made with parameters as mentioned in law. Site-specific details may require some more parameters to be added so as to find site-specific solutions for the monument as well as the community residing around it. With the examples available as above, not much variation is seen.

(8) Heritage byelaws formulated are in English and Hindi. For larger outreach they should also be available in the local language of the place where the protected site is situated.

(9) Many residences are located in prohibitory and regulated areas for long period of time. Evacuations in these areas are understood and are healthy for the monuments. These evacuations are not easy and sensitivity is required to solve ground problems especially with public. But all evacuation plans need to be backed up with relocation plans with housing, occupations, skills and sufficient funds. This is beyond the scope of ASI and yet necessary to mobilizing positivity in favor of the protection of monuments. Some mechanisms need to be in built for them.

(10) Punishment made stringent is positive of the validation but offences against the officers of the government further demoralizes the officers working under the conditions of political, administrative, social pressures and lack of public awareness and will.

4.10 Heritage, Where Is It?

The 'AMASR Act of 1958' does not use the word 'heritage' at all. It protects the ancient monument, antiquity and archaeological sites and remains. The 'AMASR Act of 1958' is not the real problem for the protection of ancient monument, antiquity and archaeological sites and remains as defined in the Act, for which it has been articulated. It clearly states the restrictive definitions of what it protects, and is still relevant for it.

5
The State Acts as per the Corresponding to the Central Act of the AMASR Act 1958

5.1   Introduction

The state governments are advised under the Constitution of India to enact a law similar to the Ancient Monuments and Archaeological Sites and Remains Act of 1958, for the protection of historic monuments, falling under Entry 12 in the State List. Thus, many states have adopted the 1958 Act to pass state legislation for preservation of ancient monuments that are not covered by the Central Act.

Many of the states in India, namely Andhra Pradesh, Assam, Gujarat, Jammu and Kashmir, Tamil Nadu, Madhya Pradesh, Maharashtra, Mysore State, Orissa, Punjab, Rajasthan, West Bengal and Goa, Daman and Diu have cognate acts and provisions. 'List of Protected Monuments of State Importance' protected by the State Archaeology Department is under the respective States Monument Act.

However, the results of the work done for the preservation of the lesser-known cultural heritage by state governments have been inadequate. This is mainly because of their responsibility has been subsidiary to that of the Archaeological Survey of India. In pursuance of their constitutional obligation, most of the federating states have enacted similar legislation patterned on the Central Act; hence, equal relevance needs to be given to the protection of the respective State Acts as they too have the equal responsibility towards the protection of built heritage in India.

5.2 Definitions of the State AMASR Acts in Relationship to the AMASR Act of 1958

5.2.1 Andhra Pradesh

The Andhra Pradesh Ancient and Historical Monuments and Archaeological Sites and Remains Act, 1990, amended in 2001.

The definition of *Ancient Monument* is exactly the same as AMASR Act of 1958. The Act was amended in 2001 where, in clause (a), (b) and (d), in the opening paragraph it mentions that for the words *"one hundred years"*, the words, *"seventy-five years"*, shall be substituted.

5.2.2 Arunachal Pradesh

The Arunachal Pradesh Ancient Monuments, Archaeological Sites and Remains Preservation Act, 1990

The definition of *Ancient Monument* is exactly the same as AMASR Act of 1958.

In the definition of *Antiquity* (i), (ii), (iii), (iv), exactly the same as the AMASR Act of 1958 (v), is stated as the same with reference to the Arunachal Pradesh state government.

The definition of *Archaeological Sites and Remains* is exactly the same as the AMASR Act of 1958.

5.2.3 Assam

The Assam Ancient Monuments and Records Act, 1959

The definition of *Ancient Monument* is exactly the same as AMASR Act of 1958.

The definition of *Antiquity and Archaeological Site and Remains* is not mentioned in the Act.

5.2.4 Bihar

The Bihar Ancient Monuments and Archaeological Sites Remains and Art Treasures Act, 1976 (i), (ii) and (iv) of the definitions of *Ancient Monument* is exactly the same as AMASR Act of 1958 except in (iii) the term *preservation* has been broadened to protection, upkeep and maintenance.

In the definition of *Antiquity* (i), (ii), (iii), (iv) exactly the same as the AMASR Act 1958 (v) is directed towards the Bihar state government and declares any article object or thing which the state government may by reason of its historical or archaeological association by notification in the Official Gazette to be an antiquity for the purposes of this Act and which has been in existence for not less than 100 years, (vi) not been listed in the AMASR Act 1958 is stated as any manuscript, record or other document which is of scientific, historical, literary or aesthetic value and which has been in existence for not less than 75 years.

The definition of *Archaeological Sites and Remains* is exactly the same as the AMASR Act of 1958.

The Act adds the definition of *"Art Treasure"*; *"Art Treasure"* means any human work of art, not being an antiquity declared by the State Government by notification in the Official Gazette, to be an art treasure for the purposes of this Act having regard to its historical and aesthetic value; provided that no declaration under this clause shall be made in respect of any such work or art so long as the author thereof is alive;

5.2.5   Chhattisgarh

The AMASR Act of 1958 is followed.

5.2.6   Goa

The Goa Daman and Diu Ancient Monuments and Archaeological Sites and Remains Act, 1978

The definitions of *Ancient Monument* is exactly the same as AMASR Act of 1958 (iv) which does not include any ancient monument declared by or under law made by the Parliament to be of national importance. The definition of *Antiquity* is exactly the same as the AMASR Act of 1958.

The definition of *Archaeological Sites and Remains* is exactly the same as the AMASR Act of 1958 but does not include any archaeological sites or remains declared by or under law made by the Parliament to be of national importance.

5.2.7   Gujarat

The Gujarat Ancient Monuments and Archaeological Sites and Remains Act, 1965

The definition of *Ancient Monument* is exactly the same as AMASR Act of 1958 but its nomenclature changes to Ancient and Historical Monument.

The definition of *Antiquity* (i), (ii), (iii), (iv), exactly the same as the AMASR Act of 1958 (v), is stated as the same with reference to the Gujarat state government.

The definition of *Archaeological Sites and Remains* is exactly the same as the AMASR Act of 1958.

5.2.8   Delhi

The Delhi Ancient and Historical Monuments and Archaeological Sites and Remains Act, 2004

The definition of *Ancient Monument* is exactly the same as AMASR Act of 1958.

No mention of the definition of *Antiquity*.

The definition of *Archaeological Sites and Remains* is exactly the same as the AMASR Act of 1958.

The definition of *'non-living'* is added: *'non-living'* used in relation to a monument or site means a monument or site, which is not being used for any religious or social ceremony, rite, worship or prayer at the time of its declaration as a protected monument or site;

5.2.9   Haryana and Punjab

The Punjab Ancient and Historical Monuments and Archaeological Sites and Remains Act, 1964

Haryana government adopts the Act of Punjab.

The definitions of *Ancient Monument* is exactly the same as AMASR Act of 1958 (iv) which does not include any ancient monument declared by or under law made by the Parliament to be of national importance.

The definition of *Antiquity* in sub section (i), (ii), (iii), (iv), exactly the same as the AMASR Act 1958 (v), is stated as the same with reference to the Punjab and Haryana state governments.

The definition of *Archaeological Sites and Remains* is exactly the same as the AMASR Act of 1958 but does not include any archaeological sites or remains declared by or under law made by the Parliament to be of national importance.

5.2.10   Himachal Pradesh

The Himachal Pradesh Ancient and Historical Monuments and Archaeological Sites and Remains Act, 1976

The definitions of *Ancient Monument* is exactly the same as AMASR Act of 1958 (iv) which does not include any ancient monument declared by or under law made by the Parliament to be of national importance.

The definition of *Antiquity* in (i), (ii), (iii), (iv), exactly the same as the AMASR Act 1958 (v), is stated as the same with reference to the Himachal Pradesh state government.

The definition of *Archaeological Sites and Remains* is exactly the same as the AMASR Act of 1958 but does not include any archaeological sites or remains declared by or under law made by the Parliament to be of national importance.

5.2.11   Jammu & Kashmir (now a UT from August 2019)

The Jammu and Kashmir Heritage Conservation and Preservation Act of 2010

The nomenclature of *Ancient Monument* changes to monument but follows the AMASR Act of 1958 (iv), which does not include any ancient monument declared by or under law made by the Parliament to be of national importance.

No definition of *Antiquity* is included.

The nomenclature of *Archaeological Sites and Remains* is not used either.

It adds many more definitions including as under:

"*Heritage areas*" means those areas of archaeological or historical or architectural or aesthetic or scientific or environmental or cultural significance including man-made and natural features and sites of scenic beauty (hereinafter referred to as "listed areas" or "heritage areas") which are included in a list(s) published by notification in the Government Gazette, by the Government, from time to time;

"*Heritage buildings*" means buildings (including artifacts), structures of historical or aesthetic or architectural or environmental significance (hereinafter referred to as "listed buildings" or "heritage buildings") which are included in a list(s) published by notification in the Government Gazette, by the Government, from time to time;

"*Heritage precincts*" means streets and spaces including those around a heritage building or a group of such buildings of which they are part and parcel (hereinafter referred to as "listed precincts" or "heritage precincts") which are included in a list(s) published by a notification in the Government Gazette, by the Government, from time to time;

"*Heritage sites*" means those buildings, artifacts, structures, streets, areas and precincts of historic or aesthetic or architectural or cultural or environmental significance (hereinafter referred to as "listed sites" or "heritage sites") and those natural features of environmental significance and sites of scenic beauty including, but not restricted to, sacred groves, mountains, hills, hillocks, lakes, rivers, and other water bodies (and the areas adjoining the same), open areas, wooded areas, points, walks, rides, bridle paths, etc., which are included in a list(s) published by the government, from time to time;

"*Tangible heritage*" means any material or physical heritage like buildings, structures, artifacts, sculpture, handicrafts, fabrics, paintings, etc.;

"*Intangible heritage*" means those aspects of culture that are non-material and abstract like music, dance, drama, poetry, living heritage like traditional crafts and cuisine and knowledge systems, folklore, spiritual traditions like yoga and Sufism, etc.; and

"*Natural feature*" means those features of environmental significance and sites of scenic beauty including, but not restricted to sacred groves, mountains, hills, hillocks, lakes, rivers, and other water bodies (and the area adjoining the same), open areas, wooded areas, points, walks, rides, bridle paths, etc. (hereinafter referred to as "listed natural feature") which are included in a list(s) published in the newspapers by the authority or Municipal Commissioner or Collector or Director as the case may be, from time to time;

This Act differs from the AMASR Act of 1958.

Before enactment of the above Act, earlier the ancient monument, antiquities, archaeological sites and remains were protected in state through the Acts – 'The Jammu and Kashmir Preservation Act of 1920' and 'The Jammu and Kashmir Ancient Monuments Preservation Act of 1977'.

5.2.12 Jharkhand

The AMASR Act of 1958 is followed.

5.2.13 Karnataka

The Karnataka Ancient and Historical Monuments and Archaeological Sites and Remains Act, 1961

The definition of *Ancient Monument* is exactly the same as AMASR Act of 1958 (iv), which does not include any ancient monument declared by or under law made by the Parliament to be of national importance. The definition of *Antiquity* in (i), (ii), (iii), (iv) exactly the same as the AMASR Act 1958 (v), is stated as the same with reference to the Karnataka state government.

The definition of *Archaeological Sites and Remains* is exactly the same as the AMASR Act of 1958.

5.2.14 Kerala

The Kerala Ancient Monuments and Archaeological Sites and Remains Act, 1968

The definition of *Ancient Monument* is exactly the same as AMASR Act of 1958 (iv), which does not include any ancient monument declared by or under law made by the Parliament to be of national importance.

The definition of *Antiquity* in (i), (ii), (iii), (iv), exactly the same as the AMASR Act 1958 (v), is stated as the same with reference to the Gujarat state government.

The definition of *Archaeological Sites and Remains* is exactly the same as the AMASR Act of 1958 but does not include any archaeological sites or remains declared by or under law made by the Parliament to be of national importance.

5.2.15 Madhya Pradesh

Madhya Pradesh Ancient Monuments and Archaeological Sites Remains (Amendment) Act 1970

The term *'mound or tumulus'* has been included as an ancient monument. (i), (ii), (iii) and (iv) are exactly the same as AMASR Act of 1958.

The definition of *Antiquity* (i), (ii), (iii), (iv) exactly the same as the AMASR Act of 1958 (v) any article, object or thing must have historical or archaeological importance and is desirable to be preserved by the state government.

The definition of *Archaeological Sites and Remains* is exactly the same as the AMASR Act of 1958.

Earlier it was the Madhya Pradesh Ancient Monuments and Archaeological Sites Remains Act of 1964.

5.2.16 Maharashtra

The Maharashtra Ancient Monuments and Archaeological Sites and Remains Act, 1960

The definition of *Ancient Monument* is exactly the same as AMASR Act of 1958 except that the definition is provided for "ancient and historical monuments" which have been in existence for not less than 50 years.

The definition of *Antiquity* in (i), (ii), (iii), (iv), exactly the same as the AMASR Act 1958 (v), states that any article, object or thing must have historical or archaeological importance which have been in existence for not less than 50 years and is desirable to be preserved by the state government.

The definition of *Archaeological Sites and Remains* is exactly the same as the AMASR Act of 1958 for ruins of relics of historical or archaeological importance, which have been in existence for not less than 50 years.

5.2.17 Manipur

The Manipur Ancient and Historical Monument and Archaeological Sites and Remains Act 1976

(i), (ii), (iii), (iv) of the definition of *Ancient Monument* is exactly the same as AMASR Act of 1958 and also includes the gardens, if any, appurtenant to an ancient monument. The Act though mentions ancient and historical monuments in its title.

(i), (ii), (iii), (iv) of the definition of *Antiquity* exactly the same as the Central Government Act 1958 (v) is stated as the same with reference to the Manipur state government.

The definition of *Archaeological Sites and Remains* is exactly the same as the AMASR Act of 1958 but does not include any archaeological sites or remains declared by or under law made by the Parliament to be of national importance.

The Act has seen two amendments till now first brought in 1978 and second in 1996. The first amendment is mainly for the language edits or insertion of missed phrases to the AMASR Act of 1958. In the second amendment, it is notified that for the words, "one hundred years", the words, "seventy-five years", shall be substituted.

5.2.18 Meghalaya

Meghalaya adopts the Assam Ancient Monuments and Records Act, 1959. Refer to 3 for more details[1].

5.2.19 Mizoram

The Mizoram Ancient Monuments and Archaeological Sites and Remains Act, 2001

The definitions of *Ancient Monument* is exactly the same as AMASR Act of 1958 (iv) which does not include any ancient monument declared by or under law made by the Parliament to be of national importance.

The definition of *Antiquity* in sub section (i), (ii), (iii), (iv), exactly the same as the AMASR Act 1958 (v), is stated as the same with reference to the Mizoram state government.

The definition of *Archaeological Sites and Remains* is exactly the same as the AMASR Act of 1958 but does not include any archaeological sites or remains declared by or under law made by the Parliament to be of national importance.

5.2.20 Nagaland

The AMASR Act of 1958 is followed.

5.2.21 Odisha

Orissa Ancient Monuments Preservation Act of 1956

The Act is same as Ancient Monuments Preservation Act 1904.

(i), (ii), (iii) of the definitions of *Ancient Monument* is exactly the same as AMASR Act of 1958 with no mention of remains of an ancient monument.

---

[1] http://rsdebate.nic.in/rsdebate56/bitstream/123456789/466454/1/IQ_221_09122010_S433_p15_p24.pdf (Accessed on 22.06.2019)

The definition of "antiquities" includes any moveable objects which (the Central Government), by reason of their historical or archaeological associations, may be necessary to protect against injury, removal or dispersion.

The definition of *Archaeological Sites and Remains* is exactly the same as the AMASR Act of 1958.

This Act is amended in 2002 but it makes no changes in definitions of what is protected under this Act.

5.2.22 Rajasthan

The Rajasthan Monuments Archaeological Sites and Antiquities Act 1961

The terms 'rock painting or sculpture of/on stone, metal, terracotta or other immovable object' have been included as an "ancient or historical monument". (i), (ii), (iii), (iv) is same as the AMASR Act of 1958 but does not include an ancient monument as defined in the Central Act to which the provisions of the Act apply for the time being.

The definition of *"Antiquity"* means –

(i) any coin, sculpture, epigraph, manuscript, record, document, picture, painting, printed matter or other work of art or craftsmanship;

(ii) any article, object or thing of historical, archaeological or artistic importance, interest or value, detached from a protected monument or collected from or discovered in a protected area;

(iii) any article, object or thing illustrative of science, art, crafts, literature, religion, customs, morals or politics in bygone ages, and any other article, object or thing of historical, archaeological or artistic importance, interest or value, and includes any article, object or thing which the state government may, by notification in the Official Gazette, declare, by reason of its historical or archaeological association, to be an antiquity for the purposes of this Act but does not include an antiquity as defined in the Central Act, to which the provisions of that Act apply for the time being.

The definition of "Archaeological site" means any mound indicating ancient habitation or any area which contains or is reasonably believed to contain ruins or relics of historical or archaeological importance, interest or value and includes –

(a) any remains thereof,

(b) the site thereof,

(c) the portion of land adjoining such site which may be necessary or required for the preservation, protection, upkeep and maintenance thereof, and

(d) the means of access thereto and of convenient inspection, repairs and excavation thereof, but does not include an archaeological site and remains as defined in the Central Act, to which the provisions of that Act apply for the time being.

5.2.23   Sikkim

The AMASR Act of 1958 is followed.

5.2.24   Tamil Nadu

The Tamil Nadu Ancient and Historical Monuments and Archaeological Sites and Remains Act, 1966

(i), (ii), (iii), (iv) of the definition of *Ancient Monument* is exactly the same as AMASR Act of 1958 and also includes the gardens, if any, appurtenant to an ancient monument.

(i), (ii), (iii), (iv) of the definition of *Antiquity* exactly the same as the Central Government Act 1958 (v) is stated as the same with reference to the Tamil Nadu state government.

The definition of *Archaeological Sites and Remains* is exactly the same as the AMASR Act of 1958 but does not include any archaeological sites or remains declared by or under law made by the Parliament to be of national importance.

5.2.25 Telangana

The Telangana Heritage (Protection, Preservation, Conservation and Maintenance) Act, 2017 (Act No. 22 of 2017)

This Act does not follow the model of AMASR Act of 1958.

The nomenclature changes to Heritage Buildings and Heritage Precincts with variation in definition. Tangible and Intangible Heritage, Vernacular Heritage definitions are added.

The nomenclature of *Archaeological Sites and Remains* gets included in the section of Heritage Sites.

5.2.26 Tripura

The Tripura Ancient Monuments and Archaeological Sites and Remains Act, 1997

The definition of *Ancient Monument* is exactly the same as AMASR Act of 1958 for monuments, which have been in existence for not less than 75 years.

The definition of *Antiquity* (i), (ii), (iii), exactly the same as the AMASR Act of 1958 (iv), is stated as the same with reference to the Tripura state government for monuments which have been in existence for not less than 75 years.

The definition of *Archaeological Sites and Remains* is exactly the same as the AMASR Act of 1958, which have been in existence for not less than 75 years.

5.2.27 Uttarakhand

The AMASR Act of 1958 is followed.

5.2.28 Uttar Pradesh

Uttar Pradesh Ancient & Historical Monuments and Archaeological Sites and Remains Act 1956

The Act follows the Ancient Monuments Preservation Act 1904.

(i), (ii), (iii) the definitions of *Ancient Monument* is exactly the same as AMASR Act of 1958 with no mention of remains of an ancient monument.

"Antiquities" include any moveable objects which (the Central Government), by reason of their historical or archaeological associations, may be necessary to protect against injury, removal or dispersion.

5.2.29 West Bengal

The West Bengal Preservation of Historical Monuments and Objects and Excavation of Archaeological Sites Act, 1957

Termed as "historical monument" applicable to the state government by reason of its historical association, considers it necessary to protect against destruction, injury, alteration, mutilation, defacement, removal, dispersion or falling into decay.

The definition of "*Antiquity*" is replaced by "historical object" defined as

(i) any document, manuscript, printed matter, picture or painting, or any movable object or any matter containing any inscription or carving.

(ii) any movable object other than those specified above, which the state government by reason of its historical association, considers it necessary to protect against destruction, injury, alteration, mutilation, defacement, removal, dispersion or falling into decay.

The definition of *Archaeological Sites and Remains* is not mentioned.

Table 1.2 List of Programmes and Schemes for Rural Development

S. no.	Name of the state	The Law	Variations in the definitions different from those in AMASR Act of 1958
1.	Andhra Pradesh	The Andhra Pradesh Ancient and Historical Monuments and Archaeological Sites and Remains Act, 1990, amended in 2001	Same definition but in 2001 the minimum age for a monument to be protected is reduced to 75 years

S. no.	Name of the state	The Law	Variations in the definitions different from those in AMASR Act of 1958
2.	Arunachal Pradesh	The Arunachal Pradesh Ancient Monuments, Archaeological Sites and Preservation Act 1990	Same definition
3.	Assam	The Assam Ancient Monuments and Records Act, 1959	Same definition for ancient monument. The definition for antiquity and archaeological sites and remains not included.
4.	Bihar	The Bihar Ancient Monuments and Archaeological Sites Remains and Art Treasure Act 1976	Other definition included is Art treasure. In the definition of antiquity included are any manuscript, record or other document which is of scientific, historical, literary or aesthetic value. Age limit is reduced to 75 years.
5.	Chhattisgarh	The AMASR Act of 1958 is followed	Same definition
6.	Goa	The Goa, Daman and Diu Ancient Monuments and Archaeological Sites and Remains Act, 1978	Same definition
7.	Gujarat	The Gujarat Ancient Monuments and Archaeological Sites and Remains Act, 1965	Nomenclature of ancient monument changes to ancient and historical monument, rest the same
8.	Delhi	The Delhi Ancient and Historical Monuments and Archaeological Sites and Remains Act, 2004	The definition of "Non-living" is added and no mention of antiquity
9.	Haryana	Haryana adopts the Punjab Ancient and Historical Monuments and Archaeological Sites and Remains Act, 1964	Same definition

S. no.	Name of the state	The Law	Variations in the definitions different from those in AMASR Act of 1958
10.	Himachal Pradesh	The Himachal Pradesh Ancient Monuments and Archaeological Sites and Remains Act, 1976	Same definition
11.	Jammu and Kashmir (now a UT from August 2019)	The Jammu and Kashmir Heritage Conservation and Preservation Act of 2010	Nomenclature changes from ancient monument to monument. No definition of antiquity or archaeological sites and remains used. Many definitions of heritage area, heritage building, heritage precincts, heritage sites, tangible heritage, intangible heritage and natural feature added.
12.	Jharkhand	The AMASR Act of 1958 is followed	Same definition
13.	Karnataka	The Karnataka Ancient and Historical Monuments and Archaeological Sites and Remains Act, 1961	Same definition
14.	Kerala	The Kerala Ancient Monuments and Archaeological Sites and Remains Act, 1968	Same definition
15.	Madhya Pradesh	Madhya Pradesh Ancient Monuments and Archaeological Sites and Remains Act, 1964, amendment in 1970	Same definition. The term mound or tumulus added.
16.	Maharashtra	The Maharashtra Ancient Monuments and Archaeological Sites and Remains Act, 1960	Nomenclature of ancient monument changes to ancient and historical monument, rest the same. Age reduces to 50 years.
17.	Manipur	The Manipur Ancient and Historical Monuments and Archaeological Sites and Remains Act, 1976	Same definition but in 1996 the minimum age for a monument to be protected is reduced to 75 years

S. no.	Name of the state	The Law	Variations in the definitions different from those in AMASR Act of 1958
18.	Meghalaya	Adopts the Assam Ancient Monuments and Records Act 1959	Same definition for ancient monument. The definition for antiquity and archaeological sites and remains not included.
19.	Mizoram	The Mizoram Ancient Monuments and Archaeological Sites and Remains Act, 2001	Same definitions
20.	Nagaland	The AMASR Act of 1958 is followed	Same definitions
21.	Odisha	Orissa Ancient Monuments Preservation Act of 1956	The Ancient Preservation Act of 1904 is followed
22.	Punjab	The Punjab Ancient and Historical Monuments and Archaeological Sites and Remains Act 1964 Punjab Act No. 20 of 1964	Same definitions
23.	Rajasthan	The Rajasthan Monuments Archaeological Site and Antiquities Act 1961	'Rock painting or sculpture of/on stone, metal, terracotta or other immovable object' included as an "ancient or historical monument"
24.	Sikkim	The AMASR Act of 1958 is applicable	Same definitions
25.	Tamil Nadu	Tamil Nadu Ancient and Historical Monuments and Archaeological Sites and Remains Act 1966	Gardens appurtenant to ancient monuments are added to the definition of ancient monuments
26.	Telangana	The Telangana Heritage (Protection, Preservation, Conservation and Maintenance) Act, 2017 (Act No. 22 of 2017).	The Act does not follow the format of AMASR Act of 1958. Nomenclature changes to heritage building and heritage precincts, tangible and intangible heritage and Vernacular heritage added.

S. no.	Name of the state	The Law	Variations in the definitions different from those in AMASR Act of 1958
27.	Tripura	The Tripura Ancient Monuments and Archaeological Sites and Remains Act, 1997	Same definitions Age reduces to 75 years
28.	Uttaranchal	The AMASR Act of 1958 is followed	Same definitions
29.	Uttar Pradesh	The U.P. Ancient & Historical Monuments and Archaeological Sites & Remains Preservation Act, 1956	The Ancient Preservation Act of 1904 is followed
30.	West Bengal	The West Bengal Preservation of Historical Monuments and Objects and Excavation of Archaeological Sites Act, 1957	Instead of ancient monument the term Historical monument is used. Antiquity is replaced by the definition of historical object and no mention of the nomenclature of archaeological sites and remains

5.3 Protection of Built Heritage by State Governments in India

The state governments have adopted the AMASR Act of 1958 for the monuments not covered under the Central Act. States of Chhattisgarh, Jharkhand, Nagaland, Sikkim and Uttaranchal have not passed the corresponding state acts.

The states of Assam and Odisha are still following the Ancient Preservation Act of 1904. Meghalaya also adopts the Act of Assam.

The states of Andhra Pradesh, Arunachal Pradesh, Assam, Goa, Haryana, Himachal Pradesh, Karnataka, Kerala, Manipur, Mizoram, Punjab and Tripura follow the AMASR Act of 1958 with same definitions. The minimum age of the ancient monument, antiquity, archaeological sites and remains for protection differ from hundred as given in AMASR Act 1958 to 75 years in states of Andhra Pradesh, Bihar, Manipur and Tripura. In state of Maharashtra it is 50 years.

Modifications and variations in the definitions of what gets protected under the Act differ in the Acts of states are Assam, Bihar, Gujarat, Delhi, Jammu and Kashmir, Madhya Pradesh, Maharashtra, Meghalaya, Rajasthan, Tamil Nadu, Telangana and West Bengal. Modifications are mainly due to additions of more definitions are added or few are deleted. It also happens because in case of Assam the Act tries to combine it with Records Act or as in case of Bihar it combines it with Treasure Trove Act.

Another phenomenon observed is the adoption of parent act when a state is carved out of the state. This can clearly be seen in case of Haryana and Punjab as well as Assam and Meghalaya.

The experimentation to protect the built heritage is seen happening to adopt to the international norms in states of Jammu and Kashmir in 2010 with changes brought in the way heritage is introduced in the vocabulary of the Act. It still follows the AMASR Act of 1958 but builds in new mechanisms of maintenance and management.

New state of Telangana in 2017 follows a different framework adopting the international as well as local ways of defining heritage in contemporary times.

Lot of efforts and dedication is required to bring in the change at state levels. Apart from the legal framework, the states lack in management and maintenance systems required for protection of built heritage. The finance and human resources for protection also needs rethinking.

6
Other Acts Aiding to the Protection of Built Heritage in India

6.1 Laws Required Towards Implementation of AMASR Act 1958

The laws required for the successful implementation of the AMASR Act of 1958 are Land Acquisition Act 1827, Antiquities and Arts Act of 1972 and Public Premises Eviction Act 1971.

6.2 Heritage Protected with Help of Laws Other than Ancient Monuments Act

There are various other acts which are not mandated to protect the built heritage of India but through various sections of the existing regulations concerning heritage mainly come from laws governing Regional Town and Country Planning and Municipal Acts in the form of development control regulations or building bye-laws, legislated by state governments. Mumbai and Hyderabad pioneered urban conservation in India, followed by Nagpur, Kolkata and Delhi.

The other acts that help the purpose are Indian Forest Act, 1927; Coastal Regulation Zone (CRZ) Regulation; Cantonment Act 2006 Environment (Protection) Act, 1986. A good example is of Champaner, the capital city famous for Muhammad Bin Begada architecture, has only 36 monuments protected under AMASR Act of 1958. Ninety percent of the site is protected under the Indian Forest Act 1927; result: priority to the activities related to forest is undertaken and heritage left vulnerable due to inadequate protection.

Large number of living monuments is under the control of Hindu Religious Charitable and Endowment Boards and the Waqf Boards.

In India, legislation and state policy at different levels of governance, i.e. national, state, regional, urban and rural (*panchayat*) levels, needs to be addressed from the standpoint of heritage; for example, the municipal laws and other legislations dealing with urban development and the role of building bylaws in the development process, which have an effect on cultural heritage. The current system has strengths as well as loopholes that can be utilized for safeguarding and sustaining the protection of cultural heritage.

6.2.1 Provisions for protection of heritage through Town and Country Act

Attempts for urban conservation are made through Town and Country Planning Acts, which follow the same pattern of central and state acts. These attempts are made for large sites needing two types of protection:

1. Area level: It could be a region, city, neighborhood, cluster or a street

2. Site level where the structure under consideration shall be considered as an entire complex with its settings and all ancillary structure making it into a complex.

Mumbai

The process of urban heritage conservation started as a part of the overall approach to urban planning program of Mumbai in 1970s. The first opportunity was an initiation of Mumbai Municipal Corporation accepting the fact that it has a responsibility for preserving heritage buildings in the city. And it relayed upon the section of the Maharashtra Region Town and Country Planning Act 1966, which empowered local planning authorities to take all the steps necessary to identify and preserve the buildings and landmarks of architectural and social value for the city. For the purpose listing was encouraged.

The Government of Maharashtra Gazette the first (draft) Heritage regulation for Mumbai in 1991 and by a separate notification the state government also Gazette a 'Draft list of heritage buildings and precincts for Greater Mumbai', a list was published having 624 buildings and precincts were identified and these were further classified into three grades. The draft had the force of law, as it was backed by the Maharashtra Regional and Town Planning Act (section 46) which empowered the state government to frame regulations to protect the state's heritage under a fairly broad definition of the term. This was followed by another Government of Maharashtra notification of Sept 1991, which set guidelines for granting permission relating building activities of the three grade.

The key elements of the Mumbai Heritage regulations that also set a standard for other cities to follow are:

1. It defines conservation to cover aesthetic, cultural, historic and social values and emphasizes on the need to undertake conservation in the context of urban development.

2. It also gave a broader definition for built heritage, which incorporated not only important buildings but also groups of lesser buildings; where the group as a whole and also large areas or precinct retained a special social-economic, cultural or traditional value that was worthy of preservation.

3. It puts forth the listing and grading of historic buildings and encouraged reuse of historic buildings. The constitution of urban heritage conservation committee comprises a balanced composition of government officials and professionals from the different field associated and specialized in conservation work.

The provisions in the heritage regulations also empowered the Heritage Committee to recommend modifications to or relaxation of any other building control regulations that may impede the objective to conserve the heritage.

Two major incentives were introduced in the final regulation in 1995, one made the 'change of use' for heritage building permissible, the other incentive was the transfer of development rights, which entitled the owner of a building to claim an equivalent amount of area in the form of TDR certificate, which can then be sold for its value in the property market.

The major issues relating to the mechanism towards heritage protection are as follows:

1. A heritage-focused legislation is needed which can strengthen protection of heritage and define 'development' in respect to the heritage structure.

2. Heritage needs to be a part of development plans and land-use maps. The efforts are in process of its incorporation but are completely legalized. Hence, still heritage is at stake.

3. Guidelines and buildings byelaws had to be specific to each precinct; at present they are not. Hence the byelaws which are applicable to the entire Mumbai get applicable to the Fort area; and the sensitivity of its importance and authenticity to integrity of the entire precinct is lost.

4. Transfer of development rights is an instrument developed as a solution to compensate the owners' loss due to imposition of conservation guidelines also fail as owners avail the development rights, sells it and the problem they as well as the heritage face remain unresolved.

5. Repair/reconstruction and maintenance grants mechanism developed but inadequate, and priorities are set at a city level and decided by the authorities, focus is not necessarily the requirement of heritage.

6. Capacity building of implement authorities still is a major task.

7. The fast growing commercialization and change in the economic value of a place is also a very dynamic problem where static solution cannot work.

8. Ownership problems including dispute in ownership persists. Abandonment of property or change in ownership only adds to problems.

9. Irresponsibility of tenants towards these heritage structures and the Rent Control Act are another problems unresolved by law.

10. Non-availability of good enforcement of building bye-laws and guidelines.

11. Lack of will and resources for equipping the area against tourism, fire, carry capacity of the area, etc., are unaddressed.

These are just the few listed ones; hence, feeling assured that it is listed and has a law under which it is protected is a false face of a real situation. The problems here are dynamic in nature and fast changing; unless these issues are resolved, the protection is not complete. The Bombay Fort area is an identified precinct with maximum structures of Grade I almost under the government ownership, still it is highly vulnerable.

Hyderabad

It has followed the Mumbai example. Under the sub-section 1 of Section 59 of the Andhra Pradesh Urban Area Act 1975, the Hyderabad Development Authority with approval of the government added regulation no. 13 in the Hyderabad Urban Development Authority Zoning regulation 1981 for the conservation of historic areas and buildings with any financial commitment on the government and Hyderabad Urban Development Authority. These also follow the three grading system and have some mechanism in place.

It has no guaranteed financial aid from government or Hyderabad Urban Development Authority; this is a very volatile situation as conservation does need money. The other aspect favorable for the heritage is people's awareness about the heritage; this is reflected in the PIL's filed. The cases range from illegal constructions, to environment-sensitive issues like filling of Hussain Sagar Lake to questioning the off location of new international airport and the road-widening scheme in the historic precincts. This also brings out vulnerability of the present heritage protection situation and shows the failure of the mechanism as well as the system itself.

The Hyderabad Heritage Regulations approved in 1995, though based on the Mumbai Heritage Regulations, included natural heritage in addition to built heritage. Its incentives included Transfer of Development Rights, waiver of other building rules such as setback, heights, etc. There was a waiver of 'Master Plan' regulations if they affect heritage sites and buildings. Changes were incorporated in 'Road Widening Schemes' to prevent destruction of heritage. Change of building use is permitted for heritage buildings if owner maintains the historic building.

Ahmedabad

In Ahmedabad, the Ahmedabad Municipal Corporation has undertaken strategic interventions for heritage conservation and development of built heritage in the walled city of Ahmedabad. The Ahmedabad Municipal Corporation has been working for the conservation and development of the built heritage of the walled city for many years. After undertaking a number of surveys, studies and initiatives, and learning from experience, the Ahmedabad Municipal Corporation has articulated the methodology of these initiatives, which can be replicated in many old city centers to conserve their cultural and architectural heritage.

The methodology that was adopted included efforts to understand the history and urban character of the old city and buildings on the past experiences of Ahmedabad, other parts of the country and abroad, identifying and sharing the concerns of the old city, building strategic partnerships with communities, various departments, agencies, elected representatives and others, and establishing a sustainable process for transformation, sharing experiences and documenting the process and the lessons learned.

Now, historic city of Ahmedabad is a world heritage site and protected by the Heritage department at the Ahmedabad Municipal Corporation (AMC).

Jaipur

The Government of Rajasthan borrowed money from the Asian Development Bank to improve the urban environment of several cities in the state. In the case of Jaipur, the steps taken so far are as follows:

State government drafted a notification to protect heritage sites and buildings and to control contradictory development through a "Heritage Committee". A heritage cell of three officers was constituted to function as part of the Jaipur Municipal Corporation body.

Basic initiatives for documenting the walled city, conducting meetings for information, gathering and dispersing the same were taken. Initiatives were made for preparing a living history of Jaipur, as part of daily attractions for visitors to the city. Various partners who had deep and practical understanding were invited from outside the city. Attempts have been made to create a common platform for different stakeholders groups and key citizens were requested to financially assist the process.

The master development plans and zonal plans in Rajasthan deal with heritage and tourism. The Master Development Plan for Jaipur prepared by Jaipur Development Authority is one such example.

Chandigarh

The importance of the city in terms of its design and its representation as a face of New India is understood but the capital is not protected or envisaged as heritage. Nor are its most remarkable buildings designated as heritage properties. There are several urban bye-laws framed right from its inception to control the townscape character of Chandigarh.

The Chandigarh Master Development Plan 2031 addresses heritage in one of its chapter. It identifies heritage zones, heritage precincts and buildings and natural features. It also gives measures for maintaining and managing the heritage.

Chandigarh is now known as a city with modern heritage. The Capitol Complex of Chandigarh is now nominated as one of the 17 sites nominated in seven countries as a transnational serial nomination for architectural work of Le Corbusier as outstanding contribution to the modern movement. This may have also acted as a catalyst for placing the heritage protection in place.

6.2.2   Provisions for protection through establishment of heritage commissions

This law primarily protects heritage of importance not covered through AMASR Act of 1958 and its corresponding acts.

The Tamil Nadu Heritage Commission Act, 2012

The following Act of the Tamil Nadu Legislative Assembly received the assent of the Governor on the 31st May 2012. An Act to constitute a

Heritage Commission in the state and for matters connected therewith and incidental thereto, to protect the buildings or premises not covered under the Ancient Monuments and Archaeological Sites and Remains Act, 1958 (Central Act 24 of 1958) and the Tamil Nadu Ancient *Monuments and Archaeological Sites and Remains Act, 1966 (Tamil Nadu Act 25 of 1966)*;

It constitutes a Statutory Authority to advise in the matters relating to identification, restoration and preservation of heritage building and in the matters relating to the development and engineering operations which are likely to affect any heritage building. It defines "heritage building" means any building or one or more premises or any part thereof which requires preservation and conservation for historical, architectural, environmental or cultural importance and includes such portion of the land adjoining such building or any part thereof as may be required for fencing or covering or otherwise preserving such building and also includes the areas and buildings requiring preservation and conservation for the purposes as aforesaid.

The West Bengal Heritage Commission Act, 2001

This Act provides for the establishment of a Heritage Commission in the state of West Bengal for the purpose of identifying heritage buildings, monuments, precincts and sites and for measures for their restoration and preservation. It defines "monuments of heritage importance" means any building, structure, erection, monolith, monument, mound, tumulus, tomb, place of interment, cave, sculpture, inscription on an immovable object or any part or remains thereof, or any site, which the state government, by reason of its heritage association, considers it necessary to protect against destruction, injury, alteration, mutilation, defacement, removal, dispersion or falling into decay.

The Art and Heritage Commission, Government of Kerala

The Art and Heritage Commission constituted under Rule 154 of Kerala Municipality Building rules 1999 shall have jurisdiction over *panchayats*. Functions of the Commission shall be to identify area of heritage and monuments to be preserved; to identify areas of architectural importance and buildings to be preserved; to identify places or streets where a particular form of a group of architectural form of buildings alone may be permitted and to prepare model plans, elevations etc.; for that place or streets; to examine architectural features in respect of any building or parts thereof or their aesthetic vis-à-vis the existing structure in a particular area or street; to advice government or panchayat on any subject mentioned above and referred to it and; to submit periodical reports.

6.2.3 Provisions for protection by establishment of the management authority for the World Heritage Sites

The Hampi World Heritage Area Management Authority Act, 2002

This was enacted to ensure sustainable development of Hampi World Heritage Area and to constitute Hampi World Heritage Area Management Authority to

(i) prevent uncontrolled development of the heritage area and commercial exploitation of the area;

(ii) cause carrying out of the works as are contemplated in the development plan;

(iii) co-ordinate the activities of the local authorities – the Urban Development Authorities constituted under the Karnataka Urban Development Authorities Act, 1987, Karnataka Urban Water Supply and Sewerage Board, the Slum Clearance Board, KPTCL, KIADB, KSRTC and such other bodies as are connected with development activities in the heritage area;

(iv) take appropriate action to protect the public property within the heritage area;

(v) promote understanding of and to encourage proper research into the archeological, historical and environmental values of Hampi world heritage site;

The Champaner–Pavagadh Archaeological Park World Heritage Area Management Authority Act, 2006

This Act is to provide for constituting and establishing of an authority to manage and ensure integrated conservation of heritage and natural environs, preservation of historical and cultural identity and also for preventing uncontrolled development and commercial exploitation of the Champaner–Pavagadh Archaeological Park and for matters connected therewith and incidental thereto.

The Majuli Cultural Landscape Region Act, 2006

This Act is to integrate development and heritage for the protection of heritage resources of Majuli Cultural Landscape Region through education, awareness, understanding of cultural significance and ensuring a sustainable and positive development trend.

The Act essentially is a legal framework for conservation of culture and heritage of Majuli Island with a focused development initiative, making provision for a core area and buffer area.

Whereas it is expedient to provide for:

- Delineation of boundaries of Majuli Cultural Landscape Region;
- Conservation and sustainable development of the resources within the cultural landscape region;
- Preservation and progression of cultural values, ethos and identification of the cultural landscape region;
- Preventing uncontrolled land use and disintegrated developmental measures of any type as understood so far as development;
- Preventing commercial exploitation, incorporation of non-indigenous techniques into sustaining traditional life style and institution.

6.3 Continuum of the Vulnerability of Heritage

Urban areas in India are vulnerable due to developmental, economic, political and social pressures and measures are required for its legal protection and strong enforcement. No single act alone can take care of the dynamism of problems related to the heritage and its conservation;

hence, a mechanism has to be developed for heritage-focused developments in these areas.

The reality is that heritage protection in India has a long way to go. Lot of efforts and thinking has to go in for the mechanisms to be developed for its legal protection, and this cannot happen unless a will towards it is developed across sections of the people right from the government to the professionals to the citizens to whom it belongs to; and the only assurance is that at least people do understand heritage though in a restricted manner and feel it needs protection.

A critical question is about quantification of heritage protection mainly in terms of adequacy. Many would argue that an official declaration/state protection under a law ensures protection, which primarily is inclusive of maintenance, preservation and conservation of the physical aspects of the heritage. Declaration alone cannot suffice to the protection. Heritage should be inclusive of geographical and cultural[1] context. Heritage protection should be inclusive of authenticity and integrity, conservation, management system including maintenance and national identity. National Identity today is critical mainly in era of globalization and universality of heritage.

---

[1] The definition of culture for the purpose of this book includes the historical, social, political and economic aspects.

7

The Future Scope

7.1 Changing Perceptions of Protection and Built Heritage in India

The notion of protection itself has undergone significant changes in the last five decades. The process of legal protection started in India in early 19th century with empowering the government to intervene in case of misuse of public buildings. By third quarter of 19th century focus has been on combating treasure hunting and regulating the treasures found in accidental digging. Early 20th century saw the focus on provision for preservation of ancient monuments, to exercise control over the trafficking of antiquities and over excavation; and for protection and acquisition in certain cases of ancient monuments and objects of archaeological, historical and artistic interest. Protection is heavily based on the paradigm of preservation and minimum intervention. Currently, protection is understood to have two clear aspects: maintenance and management. Management of heritage is inclusive of change and development. The parameter for all decisions is based on authenticity and integrity.

Ancient India on the front of 'built heritage' had been far advanced in its approach and thinking. There were architectural treatises, which established the knowledge systems towards creation of the architecture including the monumental, so were the concepts of '*punahsthapan*' and '*jernodhar*'. '*Punahsthapan*' largely dealt with restoration of the built as per the established knowledge systems, dealing with the physical aspects of the monument/structure. '*Jernodhar*' on the other hand dealt with physical as well as Meta physical aspects of the heritage. The negative forces leading to the failure of the structures were studied and analysed. Accordingly, the structure was reinstated.

The need today is to look back at our ancient knowledge and bring forth the traditional as well as architectural knowledge system to deal with the maintenance and management of the built heritage.

7.2 Efforts Towards Protection of Built Heritage in the Contemporary Times

A lot has been said and discussed about the vast realm of unprotected heritage of India. The struggle to do something can best be indicated through National Mission of Manuscripts, and National Mission on Monuments and Antiquities. The area of concern of these national missions including that of manuscripts/antiquities and commissions set up by the Government of India is that they concentrate on documentation of heritage. The works of such national missions are either in process or completed and have/will result in a database. Use of this data towards protection of heritage needs to be evaluated. If this documentation does not form the basis for long-term decision making the entire effort shall still be non-consequential. The apprehensions to its failure are more because the focus lies on quantification rather than having clear focus about qualitative aspects.

The works of ASI including its efforts to formulate the National Policy for Conservation, guidelines for the protection of ancient monuments and archaeological site and remains, heritage bye-laws through NMA are indicative of its effort towards protection of heritage under its jurisdiction. Government schemes HRIDAY, AMRUT and Adopt A Heritage are also some models developed to go beyond the understood norm of protection of heritage.

The list of protected monuments of national importance needs a serious review. The major listing is of 1904, updated to 3667 in 1958 today has 3686 monuments protected. The list of the protected monuments in itself communicates so little. It is silent on so many aspects like what is the size of the monument or the site; why is it so important; what is the physical condition of the monument/site; what are the immediate surroundings including if they have any proximity to the other monuments; are there any ancillary structure which are not protected by the list etc. It seems that protected monuments have come to an age where the proud possessions have now become a liability. There has never been a successful review of the list available in public domain. Not many new archaeological findings have been nominated to the list nor have any serious conclusive attempts made towards analyzing the list are seen in public domain. ASI has been so lost in dealing with the conservation of monuments, solving conflicts of prohibited and restricted areas and administrative tasks that once the golden 'think bank' of intellectual discourse on heritage is fast losing its research, exploration and capacities. The nature of the organization has changed from 'technical research and exploration' to 'administration'.

Academic institutes also contribute by training professionals, holding workshops and training programmes and campaigning for heritage.

Many professionals have dedicatedly campaigned and worked for heritage. Some important names in experimentation towards legal protection are Prof A G K Menon, Shyam Chainani, Prof E F N Reberio and Prof Nalini Thakur. Former Union Minister of Culture Jagmohan also intervened and executed many programmes, which are best reflected in his book.

INTACH is to formulate the charter for unprotected heritage. Its contribution has been in documentation of sites. With many chapters across country it still is a voluntary organisation. It has been contributing in its own way.

Many NGOs are working in the field. Their works range from technical aspects to social reforms through protection of heritage and traditional knowledge systems.

The 'Tourism Industry' and 'Indian Railways' are more inclined towards the sequential /thematic allocations like the 'pilgrimage sites of India', the 'Buddhist Circuit', 'The Forts of Rajasthan' etc. They also contribute in there capacity.

Yet somehow all the efforts are just not enough for the large realm of built heritage in India.

7.3   From Reality to Expectation

The Ancient Monuments and Archaeological Sites and Remains Act 1958 protects the ancient monuments, an antiquity and archaeological sites and remains. It uses its powers of acquisition, prohibition and restriction to protect what it defines under the provisions of the Act. The base information to the formulation of the Archaeological Survey of India, Ancient Monuments and Archaeological Sites and Remains Act 1958, selection of sites to the list of monuments of National Importance, and 'The manual of conservation' by John Marshal all suggest and justify that the Act has been for protection and management of archaeological sites and remains as well as for the products of the discoveries and exploration under it.

With time and advancements in the scope and nature of heritage, the perception remained that as 'Archaeological Survey of India' must be/ is the only organization of protection of 'built heritage' in India and it has continued to be with all its efforts. Hence, Archaeological Survey of India became the nodal agency for the World Heritage Nominations of India and represents the Government of India at the World Heritage Centre. The organization thus also incorporated new sciences like 'underwater archeology' in its gamut.

The expectations from the Act hence gradually shifted from the sites of archaeological heritage to the built heritage, which is based on the concepts that are dynamic and keep evolving. All the heritage of India is now expected to be protected under the Act. This invites unnecessary criticism to Archaeological Survey of India.

There is a difference in the way protection is perceived in ancient monuments and sites of archaeological remains to built heritage. The Act uses material evidence and time for its definition while the built heritage uses values as a parameter for defining heritage. The AMASR Act of 1958 uses prohibitory and restrictive mechanisms for protection while built heritage accepts change and development as a part of protection. The mechanisms for protection are different. Hence any amendments that are introduced to the current Act shall surely not address the expectation.

To address the expectations, rethinking is required in defining heritage for India and its protection mechanism.

May be a completely new law ...

Annexure 1: Database of the Legal Definition Related to the Built Heritage in Select Countries Across the Globe

The database of the legal definitions related to the built heritage in select countries across the globe was undertaken as a part of this research for creation of base datum towards analysing how various countries legally protect their heritage in the year 2011. Some analysis to it is reflected in Chapter 2.

The task was difficult due to the language barriers as most countries have the laws in their domain language. Hence finding the English translations was not always easy. Laws are times codified and difficult to interpret. Hence equally stress is given finding other sources of well-researched documents. The most helpful are

1. UNESCO law cultural database accessible (online) available at http://www.unesco.org/culture/natlaws/

2. International Federation of Arts Council and Cultural agencies (online) Available at http://www.ifacca.org/national_agency_news/2002/01/25/botswana-to-release-a-new-national/

3. UNESCO Bangkok section of UNESCO Resources (online) Available at http://www.unesco.org/new/en/unesco/resources/

4. Website on the power of culture for non-European countries (online) Available at http://www.powerofculture.nl/en/theme/policy

5. Website of the Getty Conservation Institute in the section of publication and resources (online) Available at http://www.getty.edu/conservation/publications_resources/index.html

6. Publications of Compendium: Cultural policies and trends in Europe (online) Available at http://www.culturalpolicies.net
And many more publications and research material collected over more than five years.

The database essentially contains the name of the continent, name of the country and laws for the protection of cultural built heritage. The table with the collected data is as under:

Table 1.2 List of Programmes and Schemes for Rural Development

S. no.	Continent	Country recognised by the UN	Law
1.	Africa	Algeria	National Heritage Resources Act, 1999
2.	Africa	Botswana	Monuments and Relics Act, 2001
3.	Africa	Egypt	Law no. 215 (31st October 1951) on the Protection of Antiquities, revised by laws no. 529 of 1953, no. 24 of 1965 and no. 117 of 1983
4.	Africa	Kenya	The National Museums and Heritage Act 2006
5.	Africa	Lesotho	The Historical Monuments, Relics, Fauna and Flora Act, 1967
6.	Africa	Malawi	Laws of Malawi, Chapter 29:01, Monuments and Relics Arrangement of Sections
7.	Africa	Nigeria	The Nigerian National Commission for Museums and Monuments, 1979

S. no.	Continent	Country recognised by the UN	Law
8.	Africa	South Africa	The National Heritage Resources Act, 1999
9.	Africa	Swaziland	National Trust Commission Act, 1972
10.	Africa	Tanzania	The Antiquities Act 1964
11.	Africa	Uganda	The Historical Monuments Act, 1967
12.	Africa	Zambia	National Heritage Conservation Commission Act No. 23, 1989
13.	Africa	Zimbabwe	National Museums And Monuments Act, 1972
14.	Asia	Afghanistan	Code for the Protection of Antiquities in Afghanistan (1958)
15.	Asia	Bangladesh	Antiquity Act of 1968
16.	Asia	Cambodia	Law on the Protection of Cultural Heritage
17.	Asia	China	People's Republic of China on the Protection of Cultural Relics - 1982; Amended in 2002
18.	Asia	Iran	Iran National Protection Act
19.	Asia	Iraq	Antiquities & Heritage Law 2002
20.	Asia	Japan	Historic Sites, Places of Scenic Beauty and National Monuments Preservation Acts

Annexure 1

S. no.	Continent	Country recognised by the UN	Law
21.	Asia	Malaysia	Sarawak Cultural Heritage Ordinance, 199
22.	Asia	Nepal	The Ancient Monuments Preservation Act 2013 B.S. (1956 AD)
23.	Asia	North Korea	Cultural Heritage Protection Act wholly amended by Act No. 10000 Feb. 4, 2010
24.	Asia	Pakistan	Antiquities Act, 1975 (as amended in 1992)
25.	Asia	Russia	"Federal Law of the Russian Federation of June 25, 2002 No. 73-FZ"
26.	Asia	Sri Lanka	Cultural Property Act no. 73 of 1988
27.	Asia	Singapore	Preservation of Monuments Act 2009
28.	Asia	South Korea	Law on Preservation of Cultural Heritage
29.	Asia	Thailand	Act on Ancient Monuments, Antiques, Objects of Art and National Museums, B.E. 2504, 1961
30.	Europe	Albania	"The Cultural Heritage Act No 9048, approved on 7/04/2003; amendments were made by Act No 9592"
31.	Europe	Armenia	Law on the Principles of Cultural Legislation (2002)

S. no.	Continent	Country recognised by the UN	Law
32.	Europe	Austria	Monuments Preservation Act (as amended in 1999)
33.	Europe	Azerbaijan	Culture Act of 1998
34.	Europe	Belgium	Cultural Heritage Decree (23 May 2008)
35.	Europe	Bulgaria	The Protection and Development of Culture Act
36.	Europe	Croatia	The Cultural Development Strategy (2002)
37.	Europe	Czech Republic	The National Cultural Policy of the Czech Republic 2009-2014
38.	Europe	Denmark	Danish cultural policy since 1961
39.	Europe	Estonia	Estonian Cultural Strategy 2008-2011
40.	Europe	Finland	Act on the National Board of Antiquities (282/2004, original 31/1972, amended 1016/1987, 1080/2001)
41.	Europe	France	Law 41-401 of 27 September 1941 (amended) relating to archaeological excavations
42.	Europe	Georgia	Law on Cultural Heritage (27.06.2007)
43.	Europe	Germany	Act on the Protection of German Cultural Heritage against Removal Abroad, the Copyright Law

Annexure 1

S. no.	Continent	Country recognised by the UN	Law
44.	Europe	Greece	Law no. 3028/2002, for the Protection of Antiquities and Cultural Heritage in General
45.	Europe	Hungary	Acts on Archaeological, Built and Movable Cultural Heritage were passed in 1997
46.	Europe	Ireland	National Cultural Institutions Act 1997
47.	Europe	Italy	Heritage and Landscape Codex
48.	Europe	Latvia	Latvian Cultural Heritage legislation as at July 2010
49.	Europe	Liechtenstein	Law on the Protection of Cultural Assets in 2009
50.	Europe	Lithuania	Law on Protection of Immovable Culture Heritage (2004)
51.	Europe	Macedonia	The Law on Culture (1998) Law for Protection of Cultural Heritage (2004)
52.	Europe	Malta	Cultural Heritage Act
53.	Europe	Netherlands	Cultural Heritage Preservation Act Archaeology Act
54.	Europe	Norway	Cultural Monuments: Prohibition of Exportation and Reallocation of Objects Act (1978); and Archives Act (1992)

S. no.	Continent	Country recognised by the UN	Law
55.	Europe	Poland	Act on Protection of Cultural Goods of 15 February, 1962
56.	Europe	Portugal	Portuguese Heritage Protection Law (Law 107/2001)
57.	Europe	Principality of Monaco	Principality of Monaco
58.	Europe	Republic of Moldova	Law on Monument Protection no. 1530 - XII of June 22, 1993
59.	Europe	Romania	"Law no. 422/2001 on the protection of historical monuments; Law no. 379/2003 relating to graves and war memorials ; Law no. 235/2005 declaring the historical monuments from the north of Moldavia as objects of national interest;
60.	Europe	San Marino	Law n. 17 of 10 June 1919 - Law Safeguarding and Preserving Monuments, Museums, Excavations, Antique and Art Objects
61.	Europe	Serbia	Law on Immovable Cultural Heritage
62.	Europe	Slovakia	"Declaration of the National Council of the Slovak Republic on the protection of cultural heritage No. 91/2001; Act No. 49/2002 Coll. on the Protection of Historical Monuments

Annexure 1

S. no.	Continent	Country recognised by the UN	Law
63.	Europe	Spain	Historical Heritage Act of 1985
64.	Europe	Sweden	The Heritage Commemoration Act
65.	Europe	Switzerland	Law and Decree on Nature and Heritage Conservation
66.	Europe	Ukraine	The Law on the Preservation of the Archaeological Heritage (2004), considering provisions of the Constitution of Ukraine, Land Code of Ukraine and the Law on Preservation of Cultural Heritage, regulates relations concerning the preservation, research and conservation of the archaeological heritage, and secures the right to recognize archaeological values
67.	Europe	United Kingdom	National Heritage Act 1983
68.	Europe	Vatican City	Law for the protection of the cultural heritage (no. 355, 25/07/2001) and by several rules of procedure issued by the various institutions of the Holy See in charge of heritage
69.	North America	Canada	Historic Sites and Monuments Act
70.	North America	Dominican Republic	Law No. 318 (of June 14, 1968) on National Cultural Heritage of the Nation
71.	North America	Mexico	Federal Law on Archeological, Artistic and Historic Monuments and Zones, 1986

S. no.	Continent	Country recognised by the UN	Law
72.	North America	USA	The National Historic Preservation Act (NHPA; Public Law 89-665; 54 U.S.C. 300101 et seq.)
73.	Oceania	Australia	The Northern Territory Administration Act, 1910-1953. Environment Protection and Biodiversity Conservation Act 1999 (EPBC Act)
74.	Oceania	Fiji	Preservation of Objects of Archaeological and Paleontological Interest Act 1940
75.	Oceania	New Zealand	Resource Management Act, 1991 Historic Places Act 1993 No 38 (as at 01 April 2011), Public Act Archives, Culture, and Heritage Reform Act 2000 No 32 (as at 01 November 2006), Public Act
76.	Oceania	Samoa	Samoa Antiquities Ordinance, 1954
77.	South America	Argentina	Protection of the Archaeological and Paleontological Heritage Act No. 25743
78.	South America	Brazil	A Federal law (3537/57, approved as law 3924 in 1961)
79.	South America	Colombia	Kram Dated January 25, 1996
80.	South America	Peru	General Law of the Cultural Heritage of the Nation

Bibliography

Books

1. Bakshi, P.M. (1996). The Constitution of India with comments & subject index. 3rd ed. Delhi: Universal Law Publishing Co. Pvt. Ltd.

2. Case Material on Jurisprudence, LLB sixth term, Delhi University Law Centre.

3. Cederlof, G. (2008). Landscapes and the Law: Environmental Politics, Regional Histories and Contests over Nature. New Delhi: Orient Longman Pvt. Ltd.

4. Chainani, S. (2007). Heritage & Environment: An Indian Diary. Mumbai: Urban Design Research Institute.

5. Chakrabarti, Dilip K. (1997). Colonial Indology: Socio politics of the Ancient Indian Past, New Delhi: Munshiram Manoharlal

6. Chakrabarti, Dilip K. (1999). India: An Archaeological History, New Delhi: Oxford University Press

7. Dixit, V.K., and Bedi, D.S. (2002). Jurisprudence-II. Delhi: Delhi University Law Centre.

8. Feilden, B.M., and Jokilehto, J. (1998). Management Guidelines for World Cultural Heritage Sites. 2nd ed. Rome: ICCROM

9. Jagmohan (2005). Soul and Structure of Governance in India. New Delhi: Allied Publishers Pvt. Ltd.

10. Jain, A.K. (2003). Jurisprudence Part 1,2. 2nd ed. Delhi: Ascent Publications.

11. Jokilehto, J. (1999). A History of Architectural Conservation. Oxford: Butterworth-Heinemann.

12. Lahiri, N. (1997). 'John Marshall's Appointment as Director – General of the Archaeological Survey of India: A survey of Papers pertaining to his selections, South Asian Studies, Vol 14.

13. Ray, R. (1992). Policies and Principles of Conservation of Architectural Monuments in British India. M.A. University of York.

14. Ribeiro, E.F.N. (1989). The Law and the Conservation of Man-made Heritage in India. New Delhi: INTACH.

15. Ribeiro, E.F.N. (2004). Spatial Frameworks for Sustainable Development and the Conservation of Heritage in India. New Delhi: INTACH.

16. Richmond, A., and Bracker, A. (2009). Conservation Principles, Dilemmas and Uncomfortable Truths. London: Elsevier Ltd. In association with Victoria and Albert Museum.

17. Roy, S. (1996). The Story of Indian Archaeology: 1784-1947. 2nd ed. New Delhi: The Director General, Archaeological Survey of India.

18. Sarkar, H. (1981). Museums and Protection of Monuments and Antiquities in India. New Delhi: Sundeep Prakashan.

19. Singh, V. (2004). Jurisprudence-II. 2nd ed. Delhi: Singhal Publications.

20. Thapar, B.K. (1992). Our Cultural Heritage: A Reappraisal of the Existing Legislation and the role of INTACH in its preservation. New Delhi: Raj Press.

21. Tripathi, A. (2007). The Ancient Monuments and Archeological Sites and Remains Act, 1958, Sandeep Prakashan, Delhi.

Official Publication

1. 33rd Meeting Central Advisory Board of Archaeology, Agenda and Programme, ASI, 31st December 2007

2. Executive Summary of Documentation for Inscription on World Heritage List: Majuli Island Cultural Landscape. SI 2008. New Delhi: Archaeological Survey of India.

3. Guidelines to mitigate difficulties in enforcing restrictions of construction activity in prohibited and regulated areas. ASI, New Delhi.

4. Kangla Fort Archaeological Park Team (2003). Concept development plan. Kangla Fort Archaeological Park: Charter (1).

5. List of Centrally Protected Monuments (2006). New Delhi: Archaeological Survey of India.

6. Marshall, J. (1923). Conservation Manual: A Handbook for the use of Archaeological Officers and others entrusted with the care of ancient monuments. Calcutta: Superintendent Government Printing.

7. Memorandum- Indian Council of Conservation Professionals, 2004.

8. Ministry of Tourism and Culture (2000). Report of the Review Committee on the Function of Archaeological Survey of India, (F. No. H-15/11/2000), New Delhi: Government of India

9. National Culture Fund and ASI, ASI 2000.

10. Report of the expert group on archaeology - Mirdha Committee (Approved under the Govt. of India resolution no F-14/52/82 – M dated 18th Jan 1983), ASI 1997

11. Report of the review committee on the functioning of (Approved under the Govt of India resolution no H-15/11/2000 – Estd. dated 4th May 2000), ASI March 2001

12. Shankar, A. (1997). Report of the Expert group on Archaeology. New Delhi: the Director General Archaeological Survey of India.

13. The Charter for the Conservation of Unprotected Architectural Heritage and Sites in India. New Delhi: INTACH, 2004

Unpublished Report

1. Thakur, N. (2000). Heritage of Delhi: The ground reality. Delhi: SPA Delhi.

2. Department of Architectural Conservation (S.P.A., N. D. (2001, January–May). Understanding the Cultural Landscape of Vrajbhoomi and studying approaches for the formulation of a system for Heritage management at the regional level.

Conference Reports/ Papers/ Journal

1. Gauer-Lietz, S. (2002). Nature and Culture. In: German Commission for UNESCO, 30 years of UNESCO Convention. DRUCKZONE GmbH & Co. KG. Cottbus: Germany.

2. H D Chayya, Vedic Spirit in Architecture

3. Taylor, K., Hingston, J., and Weigold, A. (2001). Australia-India update seminars: Seminar proceedings. Canberra, 18-19 October 2001, Australia-India Council, University of Canberra. Australia.

4. Menon, A. G. Krishna (1994). 'Rethinking the Venice Charter : The Indian Experience', South Asian Studies, Vol 10 pp. 37–44

5. Thakur, N. (2010). Indian Cultural Landscape, its protection and Management through Cultural and Historic Urban Landscape concepts. Landscape Journal, 24–29.

6. Thakur, N. (2011). Scholarship and Discourse in Responsible Heritage Site Management Case: Hampi. In A. Verghese (Ed.), South India under Vijaynagara (pp. 59–67). New Delhi: Oxford.

7. Spandrel, Issue theme: The Scared, Issue 3 monsoon 2011, Bhopal: SPA Bhopal

PhD

1. Nalini Thakur, August 1986. A Conservation Policy for India : An Introduction to the Context. Institute of Advanced Architectural Studies, University of York, Conservation studies. York: Unpublished.

2. Rajat Ray, August 1992, Policies and principles of conservation of architectural monuments in British India, A dissertation for M A in conservation studies, Institute of advanced architectural studies, University of York.

3. Thakur, N. (2003-2007). Hampi Integrated Management Plan. New Delhi: Unpublished.

4. Vishakha Kawathekar, June 2013, Relevance of the Ancient Monuments and Archaeological Sites and Remains Act 1958 and its applicability in the changed scope and advancements in the field of Heritage and its protection, National Museum Institute: New Delhi

Newspaper Articles

1. Singh, K. (2010). A Monument to Preservation. The Times of India, 27 July.

Bare Acts

1. The Ancient Monuments and Archaeological Sites and Remains Act 1958 (Act no 24 of 1958), updated as per the Ancient monuments and archaeological sites and remains (Amendment and Validation) bill, 2010.

2. The Delhi ancient and historical monuments and archaeological sites and remains bill.

3. The Environmental (Protection) Act, 1986.

4. The Eviction Act.

5. The Indian Forest Act, 1927.

6. The Land Acquisition act, 1894.

7. The Slums Areas (Improvement and Clearance) Act, 1956.

UNESCO Documents

1. UNESCO (2003). Operational Guidelines for the implementation of the World Heritage Convention, World Heritage Centre.

2. Architecture and protection of monuments and sites of historic interest, Series published by the German commission for UNESCO, Federal Republic of Germany, November1980.

3. UNESCO (1972). Convention concerning the protection of the world cultural and natural heritage: adopted by the General Conference at its 17th session. Paris, 16 Nov., UNESCO. Available at: http://whc.unesco.org/en/conventiontext (Accessed on 30 March 2009)

4. UNESCO, WHC (1994). The Nara Document on Authenticity (Nara Conference on Authenticity in relation to the World Heritage Convention held at Nara, Japan from 1-6 November 1994) (online) Available at: http://www.google.co.in/search?client=safari&rls=en us&q=nara+document+on+authenticity&ie=UTF-8&oe=UTF-8&redir_esc=&ei=C8rxTpXSGYaHrAfn3tDbDw (Accessed 20 Dec 2011)

5. HOI AN Protocol for Best Conservation Practice in Asia, Professional Guidelines for Assuring and Preserving the Authenticity of Heritage Sites in the Context of the Cultures of Asia, Adopted by the Asia-Oceania Region at the ICOMOS General Assembly in Xi'an, China in 2005 (Online)Available at: http://unesdoc.unesco.org/images/0018/001826/182617e.pdf (Accessed on 16 Jan 2011)

6. ICOMOS China (2002). The Principles for the Conservation of Heritage Sites in China (Online) Available at: http://www.getty.edu/conservation/ publications_resources/pdf_publications/china_prin_2english.pdf (Accessed on 16 Jan 2011)

7. World Summit on Sustainable Development held at Johannesburg on 26th August to 4th September 2002

8. UNESCO (2003). Convention for the Safeguarding of the Intangible Cultural Heritage, (Online) Available at: http://unesdoc.unesco.org/images/0013/001325/132540e.pdf (Accessed on 16 Jan 2011)

Index

73rd and 74th Amendments, 22

A

Abandoned structures, 7
Access to protected monuments, 33
Accidental findings, 15
Activities permitted, 13
Agricultural practices, 32
Allocation of funds, 13
AMASR Act of 1958, 10–11, 26, 36, 41, 43–46, 48–61, 67, 75
Ancient knowledge, 18, 73
Ancient monument, 8, 10, 23–24, 26, 41, 43–46, 48–59
Ancient monuments, 1, 11, 17, 21–23, 25–29, 31, 33, 35–36, 38, 40–45, 48–49, 51, 54, 56–59, 61, 68, 72–73, 75, 79
Ancient Monuments Act, 26, 61
Ancient Monuments and Archaeological Sites and Remains (amendment and validation) Act, 2010, 36, 38, 40
Ancient Monuments and Archaeological Sites and Remains Act 1958, 1, 21–23, 33, 36, 68, 75
Ancient Monuments Preservation Act, 1904, 21
Antiquities, 4–5, 11, 17, 21, 25, 33–34, 48, 52, 55, 58, 61, 72–73, 77–81, 84

Antiquities and Art Treasures Act, 1972, 21
Antiquities and Arts Act of 1972, 61
Archaeological areas, 5, 29–30
Archaeological excavations, 25, 31, 80
Archaeological heritage, 6–7, 75, 83
Archaeological remains or historic, 8
Archaeological sites and remains, 8–10, 24, 43, 53, 73
Archaeological Survey of India, 1, 13, 26, 32, 35, 42, 75
Architectural knowledge system, 18, 73
Architectural styles, 10
Architecture, 5–6, 18, 29, 36, 61, 72
Article 21, 19
Article 25, 19
Article 26, 19
Article 49, 20
Article 51, 20
Article 246, 20
Authenticity, 7–10, 18, 64, 71–72

B

Buffer zones, 14
Built heritage, 1–4, 6, 8, 10, 12, 14, 16, 18, 20–22, 24, 26, 28, 30, 32, 34, 37, 39–40, 42, 44, 46, 48, 50, 52, 54, 56, 58–78, 80, 82, 84
Built-in cultural rights, 19

C

Cantonment Act 2006, 61
Capacity-building, 10
Centrally protected monuments, 1, 23, 28, 35, 38
Charters, 2–3
Citizens, 19, 67, 71
Coastal regulation zone (CRZ) regulation, 61
Colonization, 4
Commercialization, 64
Conservation guidelines, 64
Conservation professionals, 3
Constitution of India, 19–21, 42
Contextual heritage, 3
Cost of maintenance, 16
Cultural diversity, 10, 20
Cultural heritage, 5–7, 11–13, 23, 27, 29, 42, 62, 78–84
Cultural landscapes, 5, 10
Cultural resources, 5, 10
Culture, 1–2, 4, 13, 19–21, 33, 40, 48, 70–71, 74, 76, 80–81, 84

D

De-gazetting, 13
Different builders, 10
Directive principles of state policy, 19–20
Dominant community, 4

E

Entrance fee, 33
Environment (Protection) Act, 1986, 61
Excavations, 15, 25, 31, 80, 82
Expert advisory committee, 38

F

Favourite political aspiration, 4
Figurative sources, 8
Fundamental duties, 19–20
Fundamental rights, 19

G

Geographical locations, 10, 29
Globalization, 2, 71
Groups of buildings, 6

H

Heritage byelaws, 37–39
Heritage impact assessment, 33
Heritage laws, 4, 11, 13, 15–16
Heritage precincts, 47, 54, 57–58, 67
Historic garden, 6
Historic towns, 6
Homogeneity, 6

I

ICOMOS, 2, 7
Illumination, 35
Indian Forest Act 1927, 61
Industrial heritage, 3, 10, 29
Information sources, 7–8
Intangible heritage, 4, 10, 48, 54, 57–58
Integrity, 8–10, 18, 64, 71–72
International peace and security, 20

J

Jernodhar, 18, 72

Index **93**

L
Land Acquisition Act 1827, 61
Language, 4, 19, 39, 50, 76
Legal management framework, 17
Level of authority, 13
List of protected monuments/archaeological areas of national importance, 29–30

M
Management mechanism, 9–10
Mining operations, 34
Ministry of Culture, 13
Modern Heritage, 29, 67
Monumental scale, 4
Monuments, 1–2, 5, 10–13, 17, 20–23, 25–46, 48–59, 61, 68, 72–75, 77–83
Municipal corporations, 13

N
National monument authority, 29, 36–37
National monuments, 1, 13, 27, 38, 40, 78
Natural feature, 48, 57

O
Ownership problems, 64

P
Paleontological material, 15
Planning control mechanisms, 9
Preamble, 3, 25–28
Principles of compensation, 25
Principles of conservation, 32

Private ownership, 14
Prohibited area, 35–36, 38
Property rights, 13
Protected area, 9, 24, 26, 33, 37–38, 52
Protected monument, 24, 26, 30–31, 34, 37, 45, 52
Protected zone, 12
Public access, 13
Public awareness, 39
Public interest, 14, 32
Public premises eviction act 1971, 61
Public records, 21
Public Records Act, 1993, 21
Punahsthapan, 18, 72
Punishment, 39

R
Recognized religious usage or custom, 34
Reconstruction, 8, 31, 36–37, 64
Repair/reconstruction and maintenance grants, 64

S
Scientific dimensions, 8
Sound and light show, 35
Spiritual beliefs, 4
State monuments, 1
State-protected monuments, 1, 32
States Reorganization Act 1956, 23

T
Tax exemptions, 16
The concurrent list, 20–21

The State list, 21, 42
The Union list, 20–21
Time period, 10
Town and Country Planning Acts, 62
Traditional technological practices, 9
Transfer of development rights, 63–65
Typologies, 10

U
UNESCO, 2–4, 11, 27–29, 76
Urban or regional planning instruments, 9

V
Vandalism, 32

W
World heritage centre, 2, 75
World heritage convention, 3, 6
World heritage list, 2–3
World heritage sites, 2, 12, 29, 40, 69

Z
Zones of protection, 14

www.ingramcontent.com/pod-product-compliance
Lightning Source LLC
Chambersburg PA
CBHW021715230426
43668CB00008B/845